Rethinking the American High School
Finding Your Focus and Using Your Strenghts

Will Dwyer and Chuck Hiscock

FIRST
Educational Resources

POWERFUL • AFFORDABLE • SUSTAINABLE

Published by:
FIRST Educational Resources, LLC
Oshkosh, Wisconsin
www.firsteducation-us.com
info@firsteducation-us.com
ISBN-13: 978-1-7332390-1-1

Printed in the United States of America
(Steinert Printing Company, Oshkosh, WI)

"This book provides both an examination and an insight of the modern American High School from two quality contemporary practitioners. The topics are thought provoking as well as reaffirming. It is a great way to create credibility and generate the right dialogue allowing for progressive strategies."

—Jeff Craig Ed.D.
Superintendent
West Aurora School District 129

"Complex challenges require complex solutions and school reform is no exception. *Rethinking The American High School* combines practical guidance with current research-based practices, resulting in a practitioners playbook for American school leaders. There is transformational potential here if the lessons on leadership, curriculum, instruction, and culture can be applied."

—Nick Baughman, Ed.D.
Associate Superintendent of Learning and Instruction
Yorkville Community Unit School District 115

About the Authors

Will Dwyer has 13 years of school leadership experience and currently serves as the principal of West Chicago High School in West Chicago, Illinois. His areas of research include principal and collective teacher efficacy. Will is passionate about social justice, student and teacher empowerment and embedding critical thinking into instruction. He serves as an adjunct faculty member at Northern Illinois University specializing in curriculum design and evaluation. He lives and works in the western suburbs of Chicago with his wife and three small children.

Chuck Hiscock has been an educator for over 28 years and is passionate about providing challenging learning opportunities to all students. He currently serves as the principal of West Aurora High School in Aurora, Illinois and as an adjunct faculty member at a local university teaching courses in School Law and School Policy.

Dedication

Seeing this work evolve from a conversation to an idea and eventually a published work has been exhilarating. A tip of my professional cap to my partner in crime and good friend, Chuck Hiscock. You've been a colleague and a mentor in countless ways. I look forward to our continued partnership and friendship.

A heartfelt thank you also goes to my former professors Dr. Mike Schroeder and Dr. Elizabeth Wilkins. You have both impacted me in ways that I will never be able to repay. To my uncle Arthur, who taught an aspiring teacher that education created choice...and to always use DAP sticky tack for posters!

A deep and profound thank you to all the amazing students, teachers, and leaders whose insights and experiences form the bedrock of this work. So much of so many of you will remain with me forever! To my parents, for instilling a love of education and sense of service in my DNA. You've been the driving force behind me in all endeavors.

Finally, to my wife Sara and my amazing children. Without your love and belief, I would not know the true joys of life. Thank you for everything you do for me and everything you make me. I love you all so much.

- Will

Writing this book has been a challenging, energizing, and at times very humbling experience...one that could not have happened without the help of many supportive people, including my writing partner and friend, Will Dwyer. Here's to many more breakfast conversations in the upcoming years!

Kelly, thank you for allowing me to pursue my passions for over 30 years, regardless of how silly some of them seemed to be. Without your love and support, nothing I have ever done would be possible. Alison and Chris, you are my reasons for being. I appreciate the many, many sacrifices you have made over the years while I spent so much time at work.

To my parents, in addition to your unfailing love, patience, and guidance, I thank you for showing me your love of reading and your faith. Those simple gifts are the foundation everything else is built upon.

To Delores, Jim, and Jo, thank you for the love and support you provided in difficult times. To Jeff Craig, an amazing superintendent, leader, and friend for more than 25 years, thank you for trusting and believing in me, sometimes more than I believed in myself. To the incredibly dedicated and hard-working people of the West Aurora High School Community, thank you for everything you do. You are making a real difference every single day.

Finally, thanks to the most unbelievable young people I have ever worked with…the amazing students of West Aurora High School. You prove every day that our country's future is in great hands! Go Blackhawks!

- Chuck

Preface

As colleagues, we became frustrated—and at times, cynical—about the way high schools were being portrayed. In our professional work, we noticed a rising desire by those inside and outside education to oversimplify educating high school aged children. We grew concerned when the call for simplification morphed into a call for radically changing the structure of high school without supporting evidence for alternative approaches (i.e., charter schools, online education, and competency-based programs). Our consternation in regards to ill-informed state and federal policy led us to reconsider the way we do business in American high schools. This book is an acknowledgement of the immense complexity of American high schools—and, we hope, a guide to internalizing and understanding high schools in a way that provides ALL students with a transformative high school education.

The narratives and examples in this text represent individual experiences one of us has had, or experiences that we have shared as colleagues. It is our hope that the guiding philosophies and supporting examples that we have formed over a combined 43 years of experience will provide a framework through which readers can ask critical questions and engage in dialogue around improvement and positive action.

Contents

INTRODUCTION

Educators have all heard the horror stories and screams for more accountability that are currently circling public schools in America. Pundits, politicians, writers, and even some scholars have insinuated that our high schools are dropout factories, that our educational institutions fail more students than not, that our standards continue to be dumbed down, and that educators have lost the battle for global economic competitiveness. This narrative fuels an implicit (and often explicit) sentiment that America needs a massive upheaval of our public education institutions to fix the problem. This steady barrage of assault would give any outsider the perspective that our schools have recently entered a state of crisis. Quite to the contrary, this rhetoric is a familiar one that has been employed for quite some time.

Beginning with the 1983 *A Nation at Risk* report, high schools have been under a seemingly endless series of reforms. These reforms have included career academies, online learning, charter schools, service learning, business models, competency-based education, social emotional programming, dual credit, year-round school, Advanced Placement, International Baccalaureate, and a host of other programs, initiatives, mandates, and ideas in the name of finding "the cure" for the American high school. For decades school leaders, politicians, and others have tried idea after idea in an attempt to solve the riddle of what will repair our high schools.

This book does not contain a simple answer to that 35-year search. In fact, it is our position that no singular answer exists to the challenge of providing high-quality education in American high schools. The only answer available is the nuanced, thoughtful, and effective use of the multitude of resources that all (yes, all!) schools and districts have at their disposal. In fact, many of the above mentioned initiatives may be a part of your answer. Furthermore, this work contends that American high schools as a whole are not the

1

barren wastelands many of those external to the field of education would have us believe. As a nation, America is profuse with pockets of excellence and pockets of horrific conditions—yet neither extreme tells the complete story of most American high schools. Like most complex organizations, the majority of high schools simultaneously contain quality, mediocrity and deficiency. This book is intended to guide educators through the process of strategically creating and articulating an individualized and continuous path forward based on their school's unique strengths, needs, and deficits.

This book is laid out in nine chapters dedicated to topics designed to focus leaders' thinking and actions in their high schools. While various tools and ideas will be presented throughout each chapter, the intention of this work is to offer thought-provoking opportunities for each reader to determine where their entry points to change may lie. Additionally, each chapter offers a glimpse into the complexities that all schools embody; the chapters do not provide step-by-step scripts of how to improve any one high school, but rather frameworks to use when determining the appropriate path to improving each reader's own school(s). Brief descriptions of each chapter follow.

Chapter 1 Summary:
How Did We Get Here?

The history and context of American high schools is rich and layered. Numerous global, national, state, and local trends have shaped the story of every high school in this country. Those external forces and their manifestations in the schools and communities across all 50 states form the backbone of this opening chapter. The research presented is intended to provide the reader with an understanding of where we in education are, how we got here, and what patterns exist in the history of public high schools. The intent of the chapter is not to assign blame for the past, but to be a source to inform future action. As Mark Twain so elegantly stated, "While history may not repeat itself, it often rhymes."

Chapter 2 Summary:
Interrogate Your Crisis and Find Your Focus

The first challenge that all high schools face is shedding the yoke of constant crisis. This is not to say that the work of school is not immensely urgent—it is. In too many communities, schools are where two-thirds of students get two-thirds of their meals. School is often where psychological and social work services are given, and it is often the only place where many children will see the only college graduates they know. This responsibility is humbling, inspiring, and worthy of one's dedication. In order to meet the burden of this responsibility, however, schools must find a way to stop operating in a frenetic state of crisis and to find a true north by which they guide their philosophical, instructional, and structural decisions. Without stepping out from under an unending sense of doom and gloom, it is nearly impossible for school leaders to look far enough into the future to create a compelling vision for their high school. This chapter offers guidance on how to examine the legitimacy of the labels that your high school wears (officially or unofficially), as well as how to determine your own criteria for success based on your community and their values. Most importantly, this chapter details how to tell your story before someone else tells it for you. This chapter also introduces four lenses to consider when viewing change in the high school setting:

A. Structural

B. Curricular

C. Instructional

D. Cultural

These components are not a hierarchy of simple-to-complex ideas or a sequence of steps to follow. Rather, these components should be viewed as critical areas of change and as optional points of entry that high school leaders can choose when designing and implementing the change process.

Chapter 3 Summary:
Structure: Why Leadership Matters

The work of improving student learning is immensely important. It is the task of positively impacting student learning that creates the challenges and barriers for many learning organizations. Too often, positive change is seemingly prohibited by resources, politics, lack of capacity, or a disconnection between perceived problems and presented solutions. It is the job of leadership to untangle and bring coherence so that positive change can take place. This chapter lays out the fundamentally crucial role leaders in high schools play, as well as how to shape the structure and mindset of the leadership team to meet the needs of the organization. This chapter encourages the questioning of things often thought of as sacrosanct in high schools and describes alternative ways to design leadership in high schools in order to focus the organization on learning.

Chapter 4 Summary:
Curriculum: Addressing the Elephant

An idealistic notion of the high school mission would be that they do the best for the most students possible. The sad truth is that many schools do the most for the students who are already the best. This reality is complicated and rooted in many societal norms that schools often reflect. As more and more schools experience rapid demographic change and find themselves serving students who are not native English speakers, live below the poverty line, or have experienced profound trauma in their lives, it is important that high schools examine the curricular structures that impact these students. In many schools, even in the most diverse schools in our country, an outside observer can see extreme segregation simply by visiting Honors/Advanced Placement courses and then visiting remedial courses. While the separation may consist of little more than drywall and space, the effects are profound. This chapter offers specific steps to engage staff and community in the difficult work of desegregating already diverse schools and creating a culture where all students are supported through a guaranteed and viable curriculum and rigorous coursework—not isolated or remediated away from their higher-achieving peers.

Chapter 5 Summary:
Instruction: Where the Rubber Meets the Road

Once a guaranteed and viable curriculum is in place, it is essential that instructional practices, or what is actually happening in classrooms, align with school goals. When cultural, structural, and curricular issues are stripped away, you are left with the essence of a school: teachers in a room teaching. Ultimately, what goes on in those classrooms is going to matter more than just about anything else (Hattie, 2008). This chapter explores both the art and science of teaching, identifies non-negotiable expectations in collaboration with staff and discusses more flexible research-based approaches to instruction that will have the greatest impact on students.

Chapter 6 Summary:
Culture: Why Collective Efficacy Begins at the Top

One of the most valuable pieces of research in the field of education is that of Professor John Hattie and his brilliant analysis, *Visible Learning* (2008; 2016), of the effect size of different factors on student learning. One of the most impactful factors to emerge from his meta-analyses of research is collective teacher efficacy. Bandura (1994) defined this term as a staff's collective belief in their ability to achieve the desired outcomes the school has established. According to Hattie (2016), this construct has roughly four times the minimal effect size for significant impact on student learning. While research in this area is in its infancy, Chapter 6 offers specific examples for school leaders to increase their own efficacy and the efficacy of their staff in order to create a positive culture for all.

Chapter 7 Summary:
The Role of Middle School

Another challenge facing high schools is that of the middle school. High schools often meet students when the gaps in their learning are largest. Too often in our educational structure, students progress through elementary and middle school encapsulated in a bubble of self-esteem and are rarely confronted with truly rigorous expectations or instruction. For many years, this was due to completely different standards of accountability at the preK-8 level compared to high schools. Students frequently experience a dramatic change in rigor and expectations when they transition into high school (Dweck, 2014). Students who demonstrate massive deficiencies in their K-8 years eventually matriculate to high school by virtue of aging out of middle school. Here, sadly, they are confronted with the realities of high school's credit-based system (aligned to college and career readiness standards) which they are ill-equipped to navigate. To change this narrative, high schools must find ways to ally with, support, and learn from their middle school counterparts. This chapter discusses how to begin an articulated relationship with feeder schools and explains how that relationship will pay unlimited dividends to any high school that is ready to rethink the way it meets the needs of all learners.

Chapter 8 Summary:
A Student Body that Perseveres

One of the greatest attributes any student can gain from schooling is tenacity. In recent years, this word and others (such as perseverance, grit, and mindset) have gained popularity thanks to the amazing works of Duckworth (2016), Boaler (2014), and Dweck (2014). Saying these words is a far cry from creating an educational structure where they are purposeful outcomes for all students. In order to meet the challenges with which high schools are constantly faced, they must become a place of possibility, a place where there is a genuine belief in self and others, and a place of actual opportunity for students. This chapter outlines specific strategies that school leaders can take to create opportunities that intentionally build the tenacity of students through the structure of the school.

Chapter 9 Summary:
Aligning ALL the Pieces to Make Real Change

This book concludes with practical advice to begin your work to meet the challenges of changing the trajectory of our nation's high schools. Readers are again challenged to assess their reality, interrogate their crisis, and determine their entry points for action based on the framework presented. It is our intention that by the final chapter, readers will have a renewed sense of purpose, clarity, hope, and direction.

1

HOW DID WE GET HERE?

The more you know about the past, the better prepared you are for the future.

- Theodore Roosevelt

Public schools have existed in the United States for a very long time, and they have been subject to criticism for much of their history. It is safe to say that overall confidence in public schools has eroded over time, and may now have reached a nadir ("The 50th Annual PDK Poll," 2018). As school leaders, it is our responsibility to both ensure our schools, particularly high schools, are teaching the skills that students need to succeed in today's competitive world, while also fostering essential traits like problem-solving, creativity, empathy, and grit. At the same time, we believe it is the responsibility of school leaders to address the sometimes inaccurate perceptions and biases surrounding our schools. The goal of this chapter is to provide some historical information, explore the origin of the public's overall lack of confidence in its schools, and then provide some examples of the positive impacts public schools can actually have. We'll begin by exploring the effect that one exceptional teacher had on a single student.

Living Narrative

Mr. Cruz taught math and coached soccer at Technical High, a large urban high school serving an impoverished city neighborhood where drugs, gangs, and crime are commonplace. Many of the school's students are undocumented immigrants and come from families whose primary language is Spanish. Jorge was a typical example of a Tech student. He and his brother came to the United States from Mexico with little more than the clothes on their backs when they were in the seventh and eighth grades, respectively. Not much was expected of Jorge when he started his schooling in his new country. In middle school, he was placed in an English Learners classroom, where an overwhelmed teacher struggled with a lack of resources, an inconsistent and unchallenging curriculum, and three grade levels of students in the same classroom. Jorge and his peers were expected to complete a couple of years of school, perhaps even graduate, and then go to work in the same local factory where their fathers toiled every day. In fact, as they entered high school, that is exactly the plan that Jorge and his brother had for themselves.

Jorge's story, however, ended differently. He was a soccer player, so during his junior year of high school, he met Mr. Cruz and the dramatically different expectations he held for both his students and his athletes. Jorge soon found out that Mr. Cruz expected excellence both on the soccer field and in the classroom. He insisted that students establish specific goals for themselves, as well as specific, detailed plans for achieving them. Mr. Cruz taught his students to aim high. For example, his goal for his soccer team was nothing less than to win a state championship. More than anything, Mr. Cruz refused to let students make excuses for failure. Instead, they were expected to learn from their mistakes and work hard to overcome them.

As a result of Mr. Cruz's efforts, Jorge, who began the school year with little confidence in his academic ability, began to see himself in a different light. He began to see himself as someone who could overcome obstacles and began to excel in the class-

room. Over the course of the next two years, his confidence grew. Under the tutelage of Mr. Cruz, Jorge graduated from high school and went on to college, where he played soccer and majored in education.

Despite his success in high school, college was a struggle for Jorge. He was shocked by the academic rigor of his program and felt ill-prepared for this new challenge. Jorge's fears were realized upon receiving a professor's feedback on his first written assignment. The paper was returned with so many corrections that the original text could barely be seen through the hundreds of corrections outlined in red pen. Jorge began to wonder if he could finish what he started. After all, he was not a native English speaker, and he had only been in the country for a relatively short time. How could he expect to compete with students who had gone to the finest schools and who had every advantage?

Rather than giving up, Jorge reflected on the lessons taught to him by his high school coach and mentor, Mr. Cruz. First, he resolved to read and write as much as possible. At the same time, he asked the professor who was so critical of his first paper to help and mentor him. Finally, he committed himself to working harder than he ever had before. As was the case in high school, Jorge ultimately succeeded, and on his last paper his professor—the same professor who was so critical of that very first effort—commented on the superiority of his work, how proud she was of his efforts, and finished by stating that he was now a far better writer than any of the native speakers in her class.

After graduation, Jorge accepted a job teaching and coaching at a large urban school district, and has been there for 23 years. He attributes his many career successes to the lessons he learned at the feet of his high school mentor, Mr. Cruz.

Is Perception Reality?

While Technical High is not the real name of their school, Mr. Cruz and Jorge are real people. Their story points out the tremendous impact educators can have on students. Fortunately, teachers like Mr. Cruz exist in schools across the country and are changing lives every day. Why then are teachers and schools so often attacked as ineffective by both politicians and the media? According to the latest Phi Delta Kappan survey, only 19% of those polled have confidence in public education overall, yet 70% have confidence in the local school their children attend (PDK, 2019). These numbers point to an important disconnect. The public generally believes public schools are doing poorly, with one exception: The people who are closest to schools—people whose children actually attend—are confident that their local schools are doing a good job.

As leaders, we must understand where this disconnect comes from, recognize how our communities perceive our own schools, and then come to grips with our actual school performance. Once we've established what our realities are, we can then rethink our high schools using a two-pronged approach. The first prong, obviously, involves ensuring our schools are providing the best possible education for our students. Specific ways to approach this task are outlined in later chapters. The second prong requires focused efforts to communicate accurate information about our schools to our communities so that they can clearly see what wonderful institutions of learning they are.

In order to rethink our schools and improve public perceptions of them, it is helpful to understand why they are seen in such a negative light. Many believe our high school structures stem from an outdated and failing "factory model" designed to provide sweatshop and assembly line workers during the industrial revolution. These beliefs are understandable. In fact, well-regarded experts like Sal Khan, Sir Ken Robinson, and former Secretary of Education Arne Duncan have all described schools as akin to factories, producing identical widgets in service to skills required in a bygone age (Watters, 2015); however, the "factory model" ascribed to the American school system is, at best, an overly simplistic view and, at worst, a gross mischaracterization of the actual work being done in American classrooms. Could many schools increase more opportunities for creativity and individual choice? Of course! Does this mean that all schools are somehow failing students with an outdated model? Of course not!

There are countless reasons for the endurance of both the "factory school" and "failing schools" myths. First, they are easily understood. Most people can readily imagine countless rows of workers laboring under sweatshop conditions and then superimpose that image over ranks of students sitting in desks while engaged in similarly mind-numbing and repetitive tasks. Second, cadres of "experts" have told us that schools are like factories and that they are failing our students. Because they are "experts," their opinions are repeated (and repeated often) as fact. Third, and perhaps most important, painting all schools with the same broad brush is easy, provides plenty of political fodder, as well as financial opportunity for those who can capitalize on the narrative. As a result the failing public school becomes a convenient straw man to be targeted in times of perceived crisis (or political expediency), and Americans ultimately lose faith in their schools as an institution.

Beginning Roots

If our high school model did not arise from the factories of the industrial revolution, then where did it come from? While schools certainly existed (and may still exist) that resemble factories, the model giving rise to myth—students sitting in rows and answering questions presented by a teacher at the front of the room—existed long before large manufacturing centers and assembly lines. Horace Mann introduced a new system of education to the United States in the mid-19th century after observing schools in Europe. While his innovations have been derided by some as being the catalyst for our current "failing" factory model, Mann's approach actually called for limiting class sizes, delivering consistent curriculum, and hiring a cadre of well-trained professional educators trained both in subject matter and pedagogical practice (Watters, 2015). Mann also saw the model as a conduit for providing a more unified set of social mores, responsibilities, and common beliefs critical to success in a democratic republic. Mann also envisioned public schooling as a way to expose students to a more unified set of social mores, responsibilities, and common beliefs that he saw as critical to success in a democratic republic (Chen, 2017).

Fast forward 150 years or so, and Americans now see a public school system that has evolved as the nation has grown. Not only do Mann's professional teachers exist, but so do a wealth of other trained specialists, including administrators, counselors, social workers, psychologists, interventionists, and nurses. As noted earlier though, a curious thing has happened during this time. As schools have evolved from primarily academic institutions into more comprehensive ones, confidence in them as a national institution has grown shaky, while people's trust in their own local schools has remained strong (Bushaw & Lopez, 2013). On the surface, this doesn't seem to make sense. Why would people broadly question the effectiveness of schools while at the same time believing their students receive a good education at their own neighborhood institution? The answer lies largely in comparisons to educational results from global competitors.

History's Impact

The current perception that all schools are somehow "failing" is a fairly recent phenomenon driven by two major events: the launch of Sputnik in 1957 and the publication of *A Nation at Risk* in 1983. In 1957, when the Soviet Union "won" the space race by launching the first satellite into orbit, the result was a collective national wringing of hands about the United States falling behind our Cold-War enemy in Eastern Europe. Schools were blamed for not producing enough engineers, scientists and mathematicians to compete effectively, so a concerted effort was made both to strengthen those areas in public schools and encourage more students to pursue careers in science, engineering, and math (Herold, 1974).

The nation reacted similarly in 1983 when the National Commission on Education submitted *A Nation at Risk* to the Department of Education for publication. The report outlined a woeful state of education in the United States and labeled schools as "failing" because American students did not perform as well as their international peers on standardized tests such as the Program for International Student Assessment (PISA) and the Trends in International Mathematics and Science Studies (TIMSS). As was the case following the launch of Sputnik, this lack of success represented an emergency requiring immediate remedy lest our country suffer catastrophic economic and social impacts. The panic is best summarized in the hyperbolic language found in the opening lines of *A Nation at Risk*:

> Our nation is at risk...the educational foundations of our society are presently being eroded by a rising tide of mediocrity that threatens our very future as a nation and a people...If an unfriendly foreign power had attempted to impose on America the mediocre educational performance that exists today, we might well have taken it as an act of war... (National Commission on Excellence in Education, 1983)

The response to *A Nation at Risk* has been three decades of school reform efforts and a persistent drumbeat of criticism, leading to the public perception that schools in the United States are failing.

Educators have all heard the stories of Sputnik and its role as a catalyst for change in science, technology, engineering and math (STEM) education, and most of us have at least read a summary of *A Nation at Risk*, so accepting the conventional wisdom related to these two turning points in public education is understandable. Doing so, however, would be incorrect. In fact, the United States did not "lose" the space race; it let the Soviet Union win purposefully (Goodpasture, 1957). President Eisenhower knew the United States had the capacity to launch a satellite into orbit a full year prior to the launch of Sputnik, but made a conscious decision to let the Soviet Union be the first to launch a satellite into orbit in order to both develop a spirit of international cooperation in space exploration and pave the way for the future use of reconnaissance satellites (Flank, 2015). The documents supporting these facts were not declassified until 1990, and the knee-jerk reaction on the part of 1950s decision-makers, politicians, and "experts" was to establish a renewed focus on math and science education in order to catch up with the Soviet Union (Bracey, 2008).

 The narrative created following *A Nation at Risk* was similarly flawed, but far more damaging. *A Nation at Risk* had, and continues to have, a profound impact on public education in spite of significant issues regarding its research methodology and data presentation. These issues lead Gerald Bracey to call the report a "golden treasury of spun statistics" (Bracey, 2008, p. 80). Rather than representing a consensus reached by educational experts well-versed in how students learn, there is ample evidence suggesting that *A Nation at Risk*'s findings were instead a manipulation of data intended to support a specific political agenda (Berliner & Biddle, 1996; Bracey, 2003). For example, the commissioners assembling the report had data from a total of nine national assessment trendlines. Of the nine total trendlines, only one showed the kind of "crisis rhetoric" required for inclusion in the final document. Consequently, the report stated that "there was a steady decline in the science achievement of 17-year-olds as measured by national assessments," but entirely ignored the lack of decline in any other subject or age-group (Bracey, 2008, p. 83). Because of these inconsistencies, some in the White House urged President Reagan not to sign the report, but others "argued that the report contained too much campaign fodder to ignore. They urged acceptance" (p. 83).

Whatever the reasons behind the creation of *A Nation at Risk* and its message that American schools were failing, the persistent narrative that America was somehow losing to other countries, and that our students could not compete on a global stage was reignited. As a result, decades of sometimes ill-informed school reform efforts grew out of the report, and millions of American students, teachers, and communities were subjected to experimental efforts that often had little basis in research or best practice. Consider the number of educational laws and initiatives that have been implemented since 1983: Goals 2000, No Child Left Behind, Race to the Top, Common Core State Standards, and Every Student Succeeds Act. All of these are heavily reliant on standardized testing to hold schools accountable for their efforts. Obligatory bandwagons have rumbled through our public schools in response. The failing schools narrative, begun in 1957 with the launch of Sputnik and continuing to this day, has resulted in unprecedented levels of school reform and has subjected both teachers and students to decades of ill-advised efforts to "fix" the problem.

The Eras of Education

Reform efforts since the release of *A Nation at Risk* have manifested in three major movements: the excellence movement, the restructuring movement, and the standards movement (Hunt, 2008). Interwoven throughout the three is a concept that could itself be called a movement: school choice. The excellence movement, prevalent in the 1980s, focused on increasing achievement of both students and teachers by focusing on the "conditions of teaching" (Hunt, 2008, p. 581). The movement represented a top-down approach that saw reforms developed at the state level and then sent to schools to implement. Importantly, many of the reforms were system-based structural reforms driven by business management models that were pressed on legislators by influential business leaders. In this model, school leaders became managers instead of instructional leaders (Hunt, 2008).

Perhaps in response to the top-down initiatives of the excellence model, the late 1980s' restructuring movement, largely driven by educators and their professional associations, came to exert influence on schools. The restructuring movement emphasized site-based management. School boards and administrators were encouraged to release more responsibility to schools, principals were encouraged to think creatively, and teachers were asked to do the same. Professional development, leadership, and improving teaching methods to engage more students were key issues, and additional accountability measures were proposed in exchange for the increased flexibility (Hunt, 2008).

The most prevalent school reform initiative during the past 20 years has unquestionably been the standards movement. This approach sought to shift the focus in education from what was being done in classrooms and schools to what was actually being learned by students. The shift seemed logical and was generally received positively. The devil is in the details, however. In order to measure student progress, targets and standards needed to be created, and then assessments written to determine if the new standards were met. Unfortunately, in the opinion of John Hunt and many others, "state standards were widely and rapidly infused into the nation's schools, accompanied by legislative mandates for implementation and assessment" (2008, p. 583). The speed of standards creation negatively impacted quality, leaving educators with sometimes poorly written, difficult to understand and often meaningless standards. Researchers have pointed to the sheer number of standards as being a barrier to teaching any of them well (Marzano, 2003).

In 1994, President Bill Clinton bought into the standards movement by signing the Goals 2000: Educate America Act. This legislation required students to show grade-level competency in English, mathematics, science, foreign languages, civics and government, economics, the arts, history, and geography (Hunt, 2008). Eight years later, President George W. Bush signed the No Child Left Behind Act (NCLB), which further focused on the achievement of specific standards. The bipartisan legislation, which received overwhelming support in both the Senate and the House, required states to develop standards and assess students in select grades annually in order to receive federal funding. The difference here was that the legislation, in promising that all students would meet high standards by a specified date, demanded accountability rather than learning, the most pressing educational concern of schools. This fundamental shift occurred because the statute adopted a carrot-and-stick approach. All students were expected to meet standards according to a specific time-frame. If they didn't, their schools would be punished. Schools who did not succeed in meeting Adequate Yearly Progress (AYP) would be faced with sanctions, including potential replacement of all teachers and administrators in the name of restructuring. In what Former Assistant Secretary of Education Diane Ravitch calls the "measure and punish" approach to school reform, the focus of schools fundamentally shifted from learning to accountability (Ravitch, 2010, p. 20).

It should come as no surprise that when nearly every school in the country was in line to be declared failing for not reaching the unrealistic targets outlined in NCLB, the law was replaced with a new one. President Barack Obama signed the potentially game-changing Every Student Succeeds Act (ESSA) in 2015. Despite the administration's previous emphasis on accountability through standardized testing, ESSA provided multiple measures for gauging student success, offered more state control of education, and actually required states to examine their testing programs and eliminate unnecessary exams (ESSA, 2015-16).

Politics and Profit

The emphasis on standardized testing that has consumed reformers since the early 1990s is worth looking at in context. While ESSA looks to reduce the number of tests students take, it still requires "accountability" in the form of standardized tests. Why do so many people insist that the answer to school success is evaluating, grading, rating, and comparing schools? There are several reasons, but primary among these are politics and profit—two familiar bedfellows twisted together in a Gordian knot that is almost impossible to unwind.

Politicians from both sides of the political spectrum continue to use fear to win elections, and countless businesses in the educational realm rely on fear to sell products and services. The only change is what Americans are supposed to fear. The Soviet Union is gone, so the target of our fears has shifted to our "losing" to other countries on international exams. Politicians run on fixing broken schools and have for many years. As is usually the case when important issues become political, facts are sometimes sacrificed for the sake of beliefs. Here is a fact that is very rarely shared: There is a relationship between a country's success on international tests like PISA and TIMMS and their Gross Domestic Product (GDP); this, however, is an *inverse* relationship. In other words, the more successful a country is on international tests, *the lower their GDP* (Zhao, 2014)! There is a reason this information is not regularly shared, and it has to do with the second strand of the knot: profit.

Educational reform is big business. *Really* big business. Secretary of Education Arne Duncan's chief of staff once noted that adoption of common standards and shared assessments meant increased opportunities for education entrepreneurs (Bryant, 2012). That reality can be seen in British education company Pearson's ability to entwine itself into nearly every aspect of schooling, including textbooks, assessment, data systems, and online programs. The company donates millions to political campaigns, pays countless lobbyists, has a seat on the board of directors at the Global Partnership for Education, and has earned hundreds of millions of dollars from school districts using its services—services that are sometimes received through no-bid contracts. In the words of New York University education historian Jonathan Zimmerman, "When the federal government starts doing things like requiring all states to test all kids, there's going to be gold in those hills. The people we've elected have created a landscape that's allowed Pearson to prosper" (Simon, 2015).

Zimmerman is not the only one concerned about large corporate influences on education. Writing at the *Savannah Morning News,* educator Michael Moore connected the dots:

> The testing business is a $2.3 billion business. But testing is not where the real money is made. If you want to pass the test, you're going to need preparation materials...the test preparation materials business surely dwarfs the testing business. This is still small beer compared to what's to come. This week the Bill and Melinda Gates foundation and the Pearson Foundation (a non-profit organization owned by, well, the for-profit version of the Pearson company) announced that the two were working together to create online curricula for the new common core standards...this off-the-shelf curricula includes the materials, the teacher preparation, teacher development, and of course, the assessments. Interestingly, Phil Daro and Salle Hampton from America's Choice, who helped draft the Common Core Standards, are heading up this development...Did I forget to mention that Pearson bought America's Choice last summer? (Bryant, 2012)

Charter Schools and the Current State of the Union

Pearson is not the only company that has grown and prospered in the name of school reform; there are countless others. In the past few years, one of the most significant initiatives impacting public schools has been the proliferation of online programs, vouchers and charter schools aimed at improving outcomes for students. Much political capital, and a lot of money, is spent creating, supporting and advocating for these programs despite very little evidence supporting their effectiveness. A comprehensive study done by Stanford University compared nearly half of the nation's charter schools with similar public schools. This study discovered that most (83%) charter schools were either no better or worse than neighboring schools (Ravitch, 2010). When business practices of charter schools are factored in, the numbers become even less impressive because the process of limiting enrollment through selective admission and dismissing students for "bad fit" can create an unequal playing field. Overall, most of the gains realized by charter programs can be attributed to this effect (Berliner & Glass, 2014).

Why have so many bought into these schools despite somewhat underwhelming results? Charter school organizations have become significant donors to politicians across the country and have created a complicated relationship between politics and education. By some estimates, the federal government spent in excess of $3.3 billion on the creation and expansion of charter schools between 1995 and 2015. Despite widespread evidence of fraud and even criminal behavior by some charter organizations, as well as the Office of the Inspector General identifying extensive waste and lack of financial controls, Secretary of Education Arne Duncan still requested a 46% increase in funding for charter programs in March of 2015 and a pathway for creating more charter schools was inexplicably a condition of Race to the Top eligibility (Cong. Rec., 2015).

Despite a lack of evidence to support the overall efficacy of choice programs, the Trump administration has continued emphasizing school choice for parents in the form of charter schools and vouchers. Secretary of Education Betsy DeVos has long been a staunch supporter of charter schools and voucher programs in her home state of Michigan, despite uneven results after more than 20 years of existence. Her family has donated millions of dollars to help create and expand school choice, often in the form of political donations. For example, the DeVos family once donated $1.45 million dollars in a single 2-month period in order to influence GOP efforts to derail a school choice initiative in Michigan, as well as $5.6 million on an effort to have the Michigan constitution amended to allow private school vouchers (Henderson, 2016). The school choice agenda proposed by DeVos includes funneling more public funding to private schools and creating more privately operated charters, while resisting initiatives requiring these institutions to meet the same standards as public schools.

How have the American people allowed a system of public education that has served the country well since its inception to become the brunt of so much negative press? Why have teachers and public schools become targets for ridicule and scorn? Why do a large majority of people believe that their local schools are "good" but American education is "bad" (Bushaw & Lopez, 2013)? The answer is simple. In order for people to react strongly, to advocate for dramatic change to venerable institutions, there must be a crisis. When a crisis happens, people become afraid. When people are afraid, they are more willing to try untested methods. After all, doing something must be better than nothing when faced with absolute disaster, right?

As we rethink our high schools, we as leaders are responsible for making sure our schools provide a rigorous and meaningful education for our students, as well as sharing the good work our students and teachers are doing every day. The following Living Narrative about Mr. España is a great example.

Living Narrative

Mr. España has been a teacher at a large and diverse urban high school for over 20 years. He teaches in both the World Language and English Learner departments, where he interacts with a wide variety of students each day. Mr. España's AP Spanish Literature class, which is largely populated by poor students who speak English as a second language, consistently has the highest percentage of AP tests taken and tests passed in his school. In fact, his classes have the highest percentage of students earning scores of 4 and 5, which indicates their deep knowledge of the material. Mr. España's success resulted in his being recruited by College Board to present at conferences where he helps train other educators on effective ways to recruit underrepresented students into rigorous AP-level courses and then help them to succeed. Mr. España is not solely interested in honors-level students, however; as someone speaking English as a second language himself, he is keenly interested in helping students new to the country (and the language) access rigorous curriculum. It is no surprise that students from his English Language Learner classes are also highly successful.

When interviewed about his students and his expectations for them, Mr. España's eyes light up as he becomes excited about how much his students can accomplish if they are simply held accountable to high standards and then supported through their journey. According to Mr. España, we have no idea what students can do until we truly challenge them. He talks proudly about students who are now scientists, engineers, teachers, business owners, and international entrepreneurs.

Describing a typical first encounter with a class, Mr. España explains, "I tell them right at the beginning...you're going to work hard! Hey, you're already here, why not get something out of it? I'm not going away, so you might as well do the work!" Mr. España constantly talks to students about effort. He also makes personal connections, demonstrates his belief in their abilities, and often uses what they are discussing in class to illustrate important life lessons. Don Quixote, for example, represents someone who always does the right and honorable thing, regardless of circumstance. He stresses, however, that it is not the content that is necessarily the most important thing students learn in his classes. "In 20 years, my students may not remember anything about AP Spanish Literature...but they will remember the skills! They'll know how to work hard, how to solve problems. They'll know how to work with other people. Those are the things they can use for the rest of their lives!"

When asked what makes him so successful, Jorge España talks about the lessons he learned as a struggling student back in high school. He talks about one teacher that had an impact on him in particular, one that stressed high expectations, hard work, determination, and goal setting. Mr. España talks about this teacher with reverence, and he clearly believes that he was largely responsible for helping him become the man he is today. Is it any surprise that this influential teacher and coach was named Mr. Cruz?

Aligning the Pieces

As we've shown, the "crisis" in education is perhaps not the dire emergency some have made it out to be. Are American schools perfect? Of course not. Can they be improved? Absolutely. Our purpose in providing this brief historical overview is not to lament the harm that has been done to our schools by ill-advised reform measures, or to throw up our hands in frustration over continued efforts to present our schools as failing institutions unworthy of our most precious resource: our children. Instead, we provide this information so educators understand the realities they face, and so they both ensure success for their students and communicate those successes to their communities. Mr. España sees anywhere between 150 and 175 students per day, not counting those he encounters as a soccer coach. He has been teaching for 22 years and has directly impacted more than 3,300 students. His mentor, Mr. Cruz taught for over 30 years. How many students like Jorge did he influence? How many lives were changed through his message of hard work and hope? Our schools are full of teachers like Mr. España and Mr. Cruz. School leaders need to celebrate them and share their stories.

Our goal for the rest of this book is to present some thoughts and suggestions for truly improving student achievement, while maintaining the creativity, higher-order thinking, and transferable knowledge that will allow our students to lead in the 21st century. Just as the general history and perception of American high school is more complicated than it may appear at first glance, so is the story of each individual school. The next chapter is designed to help readers explore the histories of their respective schools, peel away false narratives, and identify the real areas of concern, while trumpeting the authentic successes that are already in place.

2 INTERROGATE YOUR CRISIS AND FIND YOUR FOCUS

Comparison is the death of joy.

- Mark Twain

The previous chapter illustrated the ease with which educators may all perceive a state of crisis in public high schools. These perceptions have given fuel to an implicit call for the overhaul of public schooling including privatizing schooling through public funds. This is certainly an alluring narrative. If public high schools have failed our nation and are resistant to changes aimed at improvement, then why not simply throw public high schools overboard, start from scratch and see improved services? This call for a "revolution" in public education may seem a just and appropriately difficult task to change schools for the better. We argue that "revolution" or privatizing in order to wipe the slate clean on public high schools is in fact the *easy* way out with *less* promise of success. Creating and sustaining high schools that are thriving and capable of serving students and communities is long and difficult work; however, it is work that is possible and within reach of every school community. Not only do educators have the resources and tools at their disposal to improve high schools as they are currently constituted, but there is research pointing to ineffectiveness and decreased learning in many of the charter and voucher funded schools popping up across the nation (Fabricant & Fine, 2015; Ravitch, 2013). In order to set any district, school, department, or team of stakeholders on the path to success, educators must first define what success means for each high school.

How and Why We Evaluate Schools

Recently, an acquaintance asked for advice on where to relocate so they may place their children in a good school district. We were perplexed when our suggestions were immediately rebuffed based on the real-estate-website-published ratings of schools within the communities we suggested. When trying to engage this acquaintance in dialogue about the subtle and unique importance of any school, they were quick to say they only wanted to live somewhere in which the schools were a 9 or 10 out of 10 on the ratings site. After some web research, we were horrified to find that a majority of the schools in our Midwestern state are evaluated and rated by the same website (greatschools.org). Further, the site's information upon which it based the ratings was *over 5 years old* and *inaccurate*. After contacting the curators of this "nonprofit" website, we discovered that the site was really funded through real estate agencies and charter school advertisements, and that they were unwilling to correct inaccurate information.

By rating schools on a 10-point scale (1–3=*below average*; 4–7=*average*; 8–10=*above average*), external forces are reducing schools (and students) to simple standardized test scores. This creates two fundamental failures. First, simple rating systems fail to determine if students in a given school are doing well *in* the school or *because* of the school. There are certainly high schools in our society in which students receive excellent standardized testing scores. If these schools are never pressed to show *why* students are successful on these measurements, they are never forced to truly examine whether success is due to impactful instruction and programming or if success is a product of demography and effective parenting. There are many schools in our nation that, because they demonstrate proficiency in test scores, are being robbed of the motivation to demonstrate other unique student and collective school successes. Second, by overemphasizing standardized test scores in a rating system, we marginalize schools serving low-income, minority students as standardized test success is strongly correlated against these groups (Erskine, 2014; Hoy, Sweetland, & Smith, 2002; Meier & Knoester, 2017). As a society, we fail to celebrate schools that serve the most disadvantaged members of society and do not acknowledge profound growth because it may not conform to an archetype of academic success provided by mandates. Reducing students and schools to a very simple number or letter grade is a mistake. In fact, many of our colleges and universities are working to undo this same myopic version of success when considering students for college admission.

A recent white paper published through the Harvard Graduate School of Education and endorsed by nearly 50 deans of admissions—some from the most prestigious universities in our country—advocates for rethinking admissions to institutions of higher education around three pillars:

1. Promoting more meaningful contributions of students to the public good;

2. Emphasizing contributions and engagement of students across social, class, and ethnic barriers; and

3. Using a redefined outlook upon achievement that levels the playing field for economically disadvantaged students and alleviates excessive pressure other students may feel (Weissbourd et al., 2016).

If our institutions of higher learning, largely regarded as the best in the world, have evolved their thinking on how education can *truly* recognize academic success and are *de*-emphasizing standardized tests, then why do Americans still hold on to such simplistic evaluations of our publicly funded K-12 education system?

One answer is that education is complicated, and when making important life decisions (such as where to live and where our children will attend school), most parents and families look for certainty and assurance. Unfortunately, educators have allowed politicians, federal agencies and now real estate websites to define whether schools and educators are successful in the work to which many have dedicated their careers (Schneider, 2017). The first step of rethinking any school, and high schools in particular, is determining what will exemplify the success of the school and how the school will be defined.

Nearly every state in the country has criteria upon which schools are rated and evaluated by state boards of education. In most cases, these state/federal level mandates are unavoidable. This became particularly cumbersome in the early 2000s during the beginning of the NCLB era, when schools were evaluated on meeting a growth scale that would see all students as proficient by 2014. As the clock crept closer to 2014, many schools found themselves as failing to Meet Progress toward the goal of making 100% proficiency (Darling-Hammond, 2007; Jacob & Dee, 2011). For many years, this meant there were two kinds of schools: "failing" schools and "passing" schools. As time progressed and the rate of growth to 100% proficiency became tougher to meet, nearly all schools in every state were deemed as "failing" in one way or another. Unfortunately, by the time the law was reimagined as the Every Student Succeeds Act, and the labels were lifted, untold damage had been done and schools that spent a decade or longer labeled as failures were often left broken and underfunded due to the punitive mandates of NCLB and resulting declines in property values (Darling-Hammond, 2007).

If schools were being fairly graded and ranked based upon good, reliable information, there would be no issue. However, relying solely on test scores is wrong-headed for the simple fact that non-school factors have dramatic impacts on standardized test score outcomes. For example, mean scores on international tests such as Programme for International Student Assessment (PISA) and Trends in International Math and Science Study (TIMSS), the National Assessment of Educational Progress (NAEP) test, and college admission tests such as ACT and Scholastic Aptitude Test (SAT) are dramatically impacted by family wealth. Consider two groups of students who took the PISA international test for mathematics. Students from homes in the top quartile for family wealth scored a mean of 528, while students from families in the bottom quartile scored a mean of 425 (Berliner, 2017). This gap has remained consistent over time, and it says a great deal about overall school quality. As Berliner pointed out, the difference in scores is the difference between our nation being ranked seventh or fiftieth in the world (Berliner, 2017).

Schools with large numbers of students living in poverty have a more difficult time competing directly with schools boasting large numbers of students from wealthy families. This is not to imply students from poorer schools can't succeed—they can and they will—but they may take longer and are unlikely to be ready for high-stakes tests at the same time as their wealthier counterparts. Students living in poverty simply tend to come to school less prepared than those who come from more privileged backgrounds (Taylor, 2010). Students may be learning English as a second language, may not have as much access to reading at home, and may not have as many opportunities to visit museums or galleries as others do.

Take, for example, Basta, a refugee student who is a junior at a large urban high school in Illinois. He is a brilliant student who spent his early years at a refugee camp in Nepal where he sporadically attended school. Arriving to the United States in seventh grade, Basta studies hard, learns English, and is scheduled to take the SAT test. Regardless of how hard he has worked, he is still not likely to test as well as a native student from a wealthy family who has never gone hungry, has traveled every summer, and was read to every night as a child. It certainly is not fair to compare these two students, just as it is not fair to compare schools that are populated by such radically different clientele; however, this is exactly what happens every year.

To be clear, we are not advocating for the elimination of standardized testing. These tests play a role in the overall picture painted of each individual school. We are suggesting, however, that high schools find ways to define and articulate their unique excellence and their strengths to the public that include complex and truly important components of measurement that transcend state and federal attempts at simplicity. To be sure, this work is difficult and tedious; successful school outputs are not easily codified. This means schools must look inward to examine where and how their successes manifest and create strong arteries through which these stories of achievement and accomplishment are conveyed to the public. If schools allow themselves to be solely evaluated and labeled by state and federal systems of accountability, they will always fail to tell their whole story and therefore remain in a constant state of flux based on changing political dynamics at local, state, and federal levels. Exiting the hamster wheel of accountability begins with self-examination and prioritization, which are the first steps in creating a story to tell. This should be a compelling story where schools identify meaningful priorities and define their own success. The next section offers guidance on beginning that process.

Examine Your Labels

The sad truth is that school accountability measures and labels have been a harsh reality for decades in this country. This is due to shifting political and economic forces and because a comprehensive conversation about what Americans value in education as a country (or even a state) is exceedingly contentious at this time (Ravitch & Kohn, 2014). In our current structure, schools depend on states to provide the standards of student proficiency and school success. Unfortunately, states are also susceptible to frequent and dramatic change to these standards. Such change forces schools to frequently shift their focus as they lurch from one set of rules to the next, often before implemented initiatives can take shape and mature. Such movements can be disheartening because they leave teachers and school leaders with a sense of uncontrollability in their own schools. To be authentically successful in a way that serves unique student bodies and communities, schools must first question the labels they have been given by others. Consider these two questions

1. Has your high school been given a letter grade by your state?

2. Has your school been given a rating on a 1-10 scale or a label of some other kind?

If you answered yes to either of the above questions, determine what data or other information informs these labels. Are they comprised of standardized test scores? Are they compiled from ratings given by community members? Are they made from statistically valid surveys performed by reliable agencies or universities? Any of these are possible sources of information that comprise school ratings.

As a teacher or school leader, your work can begin by examining these labels and their sources before openly discussing them with school and community stakeholders. When you are ready to engage your community stakeholders, Table 2.1 provides a sample outline of questions to use in that dialogue.

Table 2.1: School Stakeholder Dialogue Prompts

<u>Directions:</u> *Use the following question categories and sample questions as possible guides when conducting dialogue with school communities to determine areas of shared values and future focus.*

Question Categories	Sample Questions
Areas to Celebrate	*What should we be proud of in this school?*
	What positive things do we do as a school that go unrecognized?
Areas to Examine	*What is a shortcoming of this school?*
	What are some areas of the school that are not discussed enough?
Focus	*What is one thing you would like to see the school focus more upon?*
	What is one thing you would like to see the school focus less upon?
Labels	*What labels does our school wear? Why do we wear those labels? Who gave them to us?*
	Are these labels accurate descriptors of us as a school?
	How does that label(s) make us feel as a school community? How do we think it makes our students feel?

With as many varied groups as possible, this authentic and crucial dialogue should be conducted carefully and over an extended period of time. Questions should remain consistent and detailed notes should be kept of all conversations so areas of overlap can be identified as they provide insight into what are likely crucial topics for school focus. Beyond gathering input, this process provides opportunity to create parent advocates for broader issues impacting schools: funding, community perception and countless other issues surrounding education. Additionally, such dialogue creates the ideal environment for engaging in shared learning so parent stakeholders can be equipped with as much relevant context as possible.

To find a viable path forward, school leaders must ensure they are questioning previous constructs that may seem untouchable. The following Living Narrative provides an example of why questioning labels is necessary.

Living Narrative

In 2018, the state of Illinois switched its high school accountability testing system away from PARCC and ACT to the SAT. The College Board, the publishers of the SAT, recommends a score of 480 on the verbal portion as the threshold by which students demonstrate college readiness on the exam. After adopting the SAT as a mandatory exam for all Illinois high school juniors, the Illinois state board of education arbitrarily decided to adopt a proficiency cut score of 540.

On the surface, it appeared that the state was adopting and holding high standards for students. This decision, however, was not grounded in research, and no clear learning-based reason for it was articulated. Understandably, the result was confusion and disappointment across the state (Rado, 2017). A small bit of digging revealed that the Illinois governor and legislature were simultaneously working on expanding state funding for charter schools and private school vouchers as part of a larger budgetary compromise. Since the vouchers are predicated on families from "failing" schools being able to access funds through vouchers to attend non-public schools, it quickly became apparent that there was a political interest in seeing more Illinois schools defined as failing. The fact that educators in Illinois were desensitized to this sad reality is disheartening.

The implications of failing to meet constantly-moving targets create an environment of constant uncertainty and change in schools and districts. This uncertainty helps drive a turnover of leadership in an effort to find someone who will address the next new crisis. School and district leaders must engage in the difficult work of quarantining these ever-changing state and federal measurements. Schools would be wise to give these accountability measures only the amount of consideration appropriate. By allowing mandated criteria to be the only means of demonstrating success, schools are *by default* accepting cookie-cutter definitions of success that are unlikely to reflect the unique needs and attributes of any one school, and which are very likely to change with little warning or research. In place of state and federal bars of success, schools and districts need to identify their *own* criteria that are valued and meaningful to their community. When those criteria are developed, schools and districts may center their work around those standards of excellence in a sustained, focused and long-term manner. The following sections of this chapter provide examples of how to determine local standards of success.

Determine Shared Values, Needs, Strengths and Priorities

Determining what *isn't* working in any high school may seem to be the logical first step in determining how and where to focus efforts. We contend, however, that it is more crucial to first find what *is* working, where teachers and students *are* succeeding, then to determine *why* it is working and what conditions or actions preceded success (Reeves, 2004). Identifying and then *understanding* what is working within a school is the critical first step upon which to start a conversation. By beginning the dialogue from a place of pride and accomplishment, school leaders avoid the trap of going into crisis mode and becoming defensive, apologizing for perceived shortcomings, or implicitly (and sometimes explicitly) blaming the previous principal, superintendent, board of education, or any other convenient scapegoat.

After determining the areas of strength in a school, leaders must follow up by asking stakeholders if these strengths reflect what the school community values. More specifically, they must ask staff members, students, and parents what they personally value about school and whether their school's strengths meet those values. If there is space between the identified strengths and the values, then you have found your areas of need. Because any list of needs could potentially be lengthy, leaders must work with constituents to focus and prioritize the needs so the work is not overwhelming and remains coherent.

If priorities of the community and the school seem to be in conflict, school leaders must adjust. They may need to rethink the ways in which they are spending their time or start to shape the perception of the school community around what they believe is important and what is not. Each situation is different, and when confronted with this conundrum, we encourage leaders to ask themselves a critical question: Is the school a mirror that reflects the community or a garden that cultivates it? The intended outcome of asking such a heady question is to determine if the school should only serve the priorities of the community or actively try to shape the priorities of the community. There is no right or wrong answer to this question, but to ask and answer it honestly provides an essential guidepost at a formative crossroad for your high school.

In some settings, this endeavor could lead right back down the path of external labels if the conversation focuses too directly upon SAT or ACT scores. If this happens, it is critical to dig deeper with your stakeholders to understand what it is about higher scores they desire. Presumably, the answer may be more opportunity for post-high school study and access to more prestigious colleges and universities. This is a wonderful opportunity to work with community members on recognizing every child as so much more than just a number on a standardized test. Stakeholders may share the belief that boiling down students' futures to a test score doesn't provide them with opportunity, it robs them of it. Such collaboration with stakeholders also offers an opportunity to discuss the white paper mentioned previously in this chapter; simple standardized test achievement is not as central a factor in top university admission as it once was. Talking honestly about test scores offers a chance to work with stakeholders on designing multiple ways for students to experience and demonstrate success in school without letting high stakes tests be the *only* determinant of perceived value.

Paint the Picture

Once you have determined values, needs and priorities the school community can embrace it is critical to determine what success in those areas will look like. *This critical step cannot be overlooked.* For high schools that have spent the better part of a decade defined as inadequate or failing, the sense of urgency to improve may seem so overwhelming that schools and their leaders may feel enormous pressure to immediately jump in and start "fixing." The long-term hazard in this approach is that when improvement begins to happen, it is often unnoticed or unrecognized because there is no consensus around what success will look like.

We both work in a school that had been rated in the bottom 20% of schools in the state. It was a sad condition, but it provided the motivation and political consensus for jump-starting numerous improvement efforts. As the years progressed and the efforts of improvement took root, our school community found itself in an interesting conundrum. While we saw improvement in some areas, we were fixated upon the areas that were not improving or not improving fast enough for our goals. We rode an emotional roller coaster three times a year when national benchmarking data came back. If we saw growth in three out of four areas, we spent 90% of our time discussing the one area that wasn't improving. It was only when as an organization we looked at *all* of our long-term data over a 5-year period that we gained clarity. We saw that while we had ups and downs, our students had improved their performance on nationally standardized tests by 11%. Schools in our district that had previously shown only one-third of their students as proficient had crossed the 50% threshold. While these numbers certainly did not represent our final destination, they did represent sustained improvement that we had failed to properly acknowledge and celebrate.

Our failure was that we had not set long-term goals by which we could determine whether or not our effort was bearing fruit. We were akin to the stockbroker who is devastated by a down-day on the market, while forgetting that over the last decade s/he had seen tremendous gains in almost all sectors of trading. Schools leaders must begin with an end in mind and realistic markers along the way to determine what qualifies as success. To do otherwise causes high schools and their leaders to forget their purpose and to dwell in the negative of which there is always plenty. Schools can begin by considering the various shapes success can take in their school. Defining success only through the lens of standardized test scores will result in missing a wide swath of students. Leaders can begin by looking to the research-based approach put forth by the School Superintendents Association, Redefining Ready. This initiative looks to create more varied and flexible pathways for students to demonstrate college, career, and life readiness. These indicators of readiness include:

- Advanced Placement Exam Scores
- Advanced Placement Course Grades
- Dual Credit or College Developmental English and Math Courses
- Combinations of Different Standardized Test Scores
- Algebra II grades
- Internship/work experience
- 90% Attendance Rate (AASA, 2017).

Armed with this framework, as well as other local priorities, schools can create their own big tents under which more students can find their own success. Doing so creates clear pictures of achievement and does not limit students to one pathway, but lets them leverage their strengths to create their own success.

Find Your Focus and Commit

In order to accomplish this work, focus is perhaps the most critical ingredient. We both have the privilege of teaching graduate courses for nearby universities. It was in one of these courses that an interaction played out between graduate students that exemplified the importance of organizational focus. The class was debating the merits of standards-based grading. Two students, one a teacher in a nearby district and the other an administrator in the same district, engaged in a passionate debate about whether this approach was effective. The administrator argued that the district had tried such an initiative, it didn't work, the teachers disliked it, the students disliked it, and the parents did not understand it. The teacher argued that standards-based grading *did* in fact work, and she used it in her own practice with great success. The teacher probed further and challenged the administrator to reflect on how long the district focused on the initiative and how many other initiatives the district had been implementing at the same time.

After some thought, the administrator admitted that standards-based grading was given little time to sink in and was abandoned at the first sign of pushback. He also acknowledged that the district had 42 initiatives working at the same time that school year, and that he could not think of a single one that was going well or had been a part of the district's plan for more than 3 previous years. The entire class (and the instructor) listened while the two employees, representing different branches of the same school district, came to the shared realization that no matter the merits of an idea or an initiative, if the focus and commitment to it are shallow, it is doomed to fail.

Once the leaders of a school have defined the values of the community and created a picture of success, it is imperative for high school leaders to next determine how that plan will manifest in the actions of the school. For those actions to have any chance of success, the school must find the willpower to focus intensely on the plan and the standard of success that the school creates.

It is the responsibility of the leaders within any high school to clear the decks of meaningless or past initiatives and to create the space for a school to commit its focus to a handful of meaningful actions designed to support the goals of the school. We support the selection of three to four goals for high schools and then aligning all work within the organization toward meeting those goals. By working with the community to determine what the school stakeholders value and setting goals based on those values, school leaders create an ideal opportunity to cancel or pause any initiatives that no longer support the intended outcomes of the school. If they don't, initiative fatigue, noise and distraction will condemn every good idea developed in support of their goals to a nebulous perdition populated by the ghosts of bandwagons past.

For some high schools and the leaders within them, this may in fact be the hardest part of setting a direction forward. This step requires the thoughtful, relentless interrogation of the school program, parts of which staff members, community members and others may passionately defend. School leaders must move delicately and considerately in this process. While Chapter 3 will explore in-depth examples of how to take on this difficult but crucial work, we recommend adopting two guiding principles.

Guiding Principle 1: Lay the Foundation

Ensure that you have undertaken the work of the previous section by engaging your community in determining values, needs and priorities. Make sure you have achieved consensus with stakeholders that the identified priorities are worthy of your school, that corresponding goals are purposeful and feasible, and that you will have their support in pursuing them. Gaining this consensus arms school leaders with a clear and powerful rationale for scrutinizing, and maybe even eliminating a program that is no longer aligned to school priorities. Without this rationale navigating one's actions, there is a strong chance that decisions made by leadership will be perceived as personal vendettas or political agendas not connected to larger and more altruistic intentions.

Guiding Principle 2: Three Key Traits

Proceed with complete *honesty, transparency*, and *empathy*. Education is a *people* business. When narrowing the focus of a school and letting go of past practices or programs, you will inevitably impact people. This can only be done effectively if the leaders endeavoring to do so operate with honesty and transparency about their motives: how and why they believe their decisions and plans will improve the organization. Most importantly, leaders must undertake this process with empathy toward those who are being impacted. Seeking to understand why some people may react passionately or feel a sense of loss is critical to the success of creating the conditions of focus within the school. Proceeding with these three virtues in mind will build trust and respect in the future, when it will be needed to sustain the focus of the organization.

Aligning the Pieces

The many external forces and resulting changes in the landscape of education have created daunting challenges for every high school. The way forward is not to continue playing the game of accountability and hoping the rules change in your favor. Rather, we propose schools create their *own* vision of success, find their *own* focus and commit wholly to their *own* path. The opening chapters of this book have provided the historical context that has contributed to the challenging reality many high schools are faced with today. Additionally, we have proposed the beginning steps of defining and then creating your own individual success with the support and buy in of your school community. The following four chapters present four lenses through which to view the improvement process of your school:

- Structures
- Curriculum
- Instruction
- Culture

Each chapter offers a different entry point to improvement as well as frameworks through which to view the change process in your school. We encourage readers to view these chapters as opportunities to provoke your own unique plans and areas of focus, not as linear steps in a rote process.

3 STRUCTURE: WHY LEADERSHIP MATTERS

Leadership rests not only upon ability, not only upon capacity—having the capacity to lead is not enough. The leader must be willing to use it. His leadership is then based on truth and character. There must be truth in the purpose and will power in the character.

- Vince Lombardi

Through a series of questions and examples, the goal of this chapter is to examine the leadership structure of your organization to ensure it best suits the needs of your unique school. The work outlined in the previous chapter is difficult. In fact, rethinking a venerable institution like the public high school is a daunting task. Rather, rethinking high school and then *changing* it is a daunting task. In reality, thinking about the change isn't daunting at all! Talking about changing isn't difficult either. We know talk is cheap, and any number of leaders have talked about changing and improving schools, sometimes with little to show for it. This is due to several factors. Sometimes educational leaders do nothing but talk and thereby accomplish nothing. At other times, leaders implement dramatic change initiatives and programs within their schools, but end up with the same result: little improvement in either student achievement or in school culture. In many ways, the leader that initiates an ill-advised or poorly-thought out change does more damage than the one who does nothing at all. Well-intentioned, yet misguided initiatives only perpetuate the "this too shall pass" mentality that many veteran teachers adopt in response to suffering through poor implementation of each new bright idea. There is no escaping the fact that re-imagining and then transforming your high school into one that matches the needs of your community will make some people uncomfortable, angry, or resentful.

A Word on Leadership

Leadership is a tricky thing. Numerous studies have been done on what makes an effective leader, and there is no single magical trait that guarantees success (Bohlman and Deal, 2003). Of course, educators have all experienced working with good leaders and probably all worked with leaders that were less than effective.

So what makes a *good* leader? Is it a personality trait? Probably not (De-Pree, 1989). There are effective leaders who are outgoing, but there are also great leaders who are more reserved. Some spectacular leaders have huge personalities. Others are milder. Many effective leaders are well-liked, but there are plenty of very good leaders who are not. Perhaps it is easier to identify what attributes *ineffective* leaders have in common. We will do so by sharing a Living Narrative of Dr. B., an amalgam of principals and other administrators we've encountered over the years.

Living Narrative

Dr. B. is the principal of a large urban high school where over 350 staff members work hard to provide an excellent education to almost 4,000 students. After attending a conference about a new reading program and its impact on high poverty schools, Dr. B. decides to look into purchasing the program in an effort to improve outcomes for her school. She tasks her Assistant Principal for Teaching and Learning, Ms. M., to examine the feasibility and costs. Two weeks later, prior to Ms. M. completing her report, Dr. B. sends a group of eight teachers and administrators to visit a school that has just adopted the new program. The school is out of state, so transportation, lodging, and sub costs are incurred. Dr. B. is impressed with what she sees on the trip, so upon the group's return, she instructs Ms. M. to launch the initiative. Because this will be a school-wide initiative, Dr. B shares the news with her administrative team. Department chairs and lead-teachers are instructed to share the information with their departments.

Ms. M. begins getting information on costs. As it turns out, the purchase of the program itself is only the tip of the iceberg. Additional purchases of software, workbooks, and supplemental materials are required, as is the replacement of older laptops and other devices. A committee is formed to determine what materials are actually essential, and what kind of devices would be most effective based on the district's financial situation. The committee meets three times and prepares a recommendation for Dr. B.'s review. In the meantime, the School Improvement Committee plans spring and summer professional development with the new initiative in mind. Teachers express excitement that all students will receive a consistent message and approach to improving reading fluency and understanding.

Ms. M. shares projected costs, which are higher than anticipated. Dr. B. is stunned by the budgetary impact and decides the costs are prohibitive. At the next administrative meeting she tells the team the initiative is off the table, but it may be pursued at another time. Lead teachers return to their departments and share the bad news. Staff members who were on the School Improvement Committee express frustration that the work they've already done has been wasted. As this is happening, Dr. B. contacts a charitable organization in the district that indicates they may be willing to fund the reading project.

Dr. B. returns to her team and tells them the project is back on! The cycle begins again. Lead teachers and department chairs return to their staffs and share the news that the reading initiative is once again in the offing for the following year. Ms. M. puts together purchase orders, arranges training with the company, and recruits volunteers to become leaders in a "train the trainer model."

> *In early April, the charitable organization lets Dr. B. know that they have received some negative press regarding favoritism toward her school, and that they won't be able to fund the project as they don't have the funds to support a similar program at the other local high school. When the charitable organization's funds dry up, Dr. B. again tells her team to pull the plug. Administrators, teacher teams, and department heads (whose plan for the upcoming teacher institute were all based on the new reading program) scramble to adjust. When two department chairs complain, they are removed from their positions.*

After reading this scenario, which is based on a synthesis of actual events, you may be telling yourself that Dr. B. is simply incompetent or maybe just not very bright. You would be wrong on both counts. The leaders that Dr. B. is based on were all very intelligent people running excellent schools with large budgets in supportive communities. But the result of their leadership in each and every case was a loss of trust in administration, resistance to change, and a culture of fear. Why did their programs invariably fail? Let's look to their avatar, Dr. B., for answers.

First, she had no long-term plan or vision. Dr. B. did not seek any input other than her own. There was never any effort made to explore options, build consensus, explore the needs and values of the community, or look at the new programs within the framework of her school's mission and long-term plan. Instead, Dr. B. often pursued the magic bullet, the next big thing, that *one answer* that would change everything for the better. As a result, every year a new initiative was introduced. These new initiatives usually had no connection to the previous year's focus, and the lack of continuity caused confusion and anxiety for everyone in the school. Administrators and teachers alike felt like rudderless ships, completely out of control with no opportunity to pilot themselves to a safe harbor.

Second, Dr. B. made snap decisions based solely on her own reasoning. She very rarely took advice from her team, and when she did, she often changed direction unilaterally. This approach caused the waste of valuable resources, including that most valuable commodity: people's time. Finally, while Dr. B. rarely sought input from her staff, she punished those who disagreed with her or questioned her decisions. This was perhaps her most damaging characteristic, as it created distrust toward and among people in the organization. Administrators, trying to curry favor with their fickle leader, would speak ill of their colleagues and occasionally undermine them in an effort to improve their own standing. Trust was non-existent, and finger-pointing was rampant.

This illustration is not intended to cast aspersions upon any one leader, but rather to draw attention to fundamental qualities necessary to effectively lead major changes in an organization. Consider the epigraph found at the head of this chapter. Vince Lombardi's words boil effective leadership down to its most basic tenets: the capacity to lead, the will to do so, truth of purpose, and character. Wouldn't schools be much more effective places if *all* of their leaders strongly demonstrated these four things?

This leads us to a question that is absolutely critical to success: What kind of leader are *you*?

What Kind of Leader Are You?

The accessibility of information in the modern age has led to an explosion in the amount of reading material available describing leadership. There are countless books, articles, websites, blogs and consultants devoted entirely to the topic of what makes people effective leaders. Each author, blogger or consultant may have his or her own description of the types of leader you may be.

Are you an authentic leader, an autocratic leader, or a laissez-faire leader? If none of these fit, perhaps you are a transformational leader, or maybe a transactional leader. A bureaucratic leader? Charismatic? Participative, directive, supportive, or achievement oriented? Is it important to understand what the research says about leadership? Certainly! Is it necessary to slap a label on yourself (or on your leadership team) to identify exactly what kind of leader you are? Absolutely not. Here's why: *It doesn't really matter!*

We are not saying that your leadership style doesn't matter; it does. But what really matters is whether you are self-aware enough to recognize your leadership tendencies, use them to improve your organization, and build upon your strengths. Of equal, or perhaps greater importance, is whether you can also recognize your weaknesses and then adjust to overcome them.

We make this statement with a qualification: you, as the leader, are incapable of single-handedly transforming your school. If you try and go it alone, you will very likely fail. Bohlman and Deal framed this reality perfectly when they wrote:

> In story and myth, leaders are often lonely heroes and itinerant warriors, wed only to their honor and their cause...But traditional notions of solitary, heroic leaders can lead us to focus too much on individuals and too little on the stage where they play their parts. (Bohlman & Deal, 2003, p.338)

No single person is capable of transforming a school all by him or herself, so perhaps the most important function of a leader is figuring out when *not* to lead. What, then, does the effective leader do? He or she sets the vision and then cultivates the environment and the leaders in which the whole organization can follow.

Just as schools must do the hard work of self-reflection and examination, a good leader should seek to understand his or her style and should honestly identify strengths and weaknesses. He or she should then ask others who have worked closely with them to do the same thing (anonymously if necessary). Bruised egos aside, the exercise can open a window onto your style that would otherwise remain closed. The following Living Narrative provides an example of how to engage in reflection upon your leadership.

Living Narrative

Early in his administrative career, a young assistant high school principal conducted an exit interview with a secretary that was leaving the school in order to be with her daughter out of state. The administrator had learned of this practice in a graduate class and was going through it as a rote exercise, expecting only platitudes from his soon to be ex-employee. To say he was surprised by the actual conversation would be an understatement. While the secretary had generally good things to say, she was quite frank, letting her former boss know that he needed to be tougher and to stop avoiding difficult conversations with people who were not doing their jobs as well as they could. She also let him know that he needed to communicate better and get organized.

The young assistant principal was initially hurt by the honest feedback given; however, he did not sulk about it, but instead created a survey and gave it to all of the people he supervised. He also solicited the same information from the teaching staff, as well as the building administrative team. It should be no surprise that the themes recognized by his secretary were not unique to her. In response, the administrator committed himself to strengthening those areas by attending a workshop on effective organization, writing specific goals, and developing an action plan to remedy communication deficiencies and bolster his willingness to have the difficult conversations necessary to be an effective leader. The situation improved almost immediately, especially in the areas of organization and communication. Tackling his aversion to difficult conversations was more difficult. No one likes meeting with people to discuss their deficiencies, but by recognizing the importance of holding people accountable, and committing to doing so, this too became easier. In fact, the young administrator found that holding people who were not meeting expectations accountable was actually welcomed by staff.

Recognizing his strengths and weaknesses as a leader truly transformed the young administrator's practice and made him more effective, even though he still struggles at times in some of these areas.

The second reason it is critical for leaders to examine their leadership style is that doing so is the only way to create an administrative team that is as strong as possible. As stated previously, leaders attempting to do everything themselves are unlikely to meet with the success they want. We firmly believe in the power of collaboration and the notion that several minds are much stronger than one. If those minds all think exactly the same way, however, the team will suffer from tunnel vision and will never reach its full potential. Leaders should choose their teams wisely, or commit to working with already-hired staff to identify where each person is strong and adjust roles accordingly. For example, consider a high school principal who is very detail-oriented, well-versed in research, and outstanding in instructional best practice, but who is not as comfortable with interpersonal relationships. He or she needs someone on the team who understands people and is given the freedom to manage messaging, communication and developing opportunities for collaboration among the staff. A principal who is outstanding with "big picture" ideas and adept at connecting with people, but who struggles with organization and details, should look for an organized, operationally-gifted team member and then give that person the freedom to make decisions in these areas.

If positive team dynamics and purposeful change are to take place, the negative culture described in the Dr. B. Living Narrative cannot be allowed to exist. Such cultures are antithetical to success. In contrast, imagine a leadership team where each person at the table is free to express an idea, is genuinely listened to and is given the authority to make decisions in support of the school vision without fear of being blamed if things don't go well. Which environment would *you* rather work in?

As we transition into some thoughts on how to adjust the leadership structure of your high school, we would like to underscore the need for superintendents, principals, administrators and teacher leaders to purposefully develop and nurture leadership in others. For example, as Michael Fullan stated in his book *The Principal*, the role of the principal as an instructional leader is problematic:

> The current concept of what principals should do is either confusing (What exactly does instructional leadership mean anyway?), too narrow (What is being neglected as we become preoccupied by classroom instruction?), too tedious (checklists, checklists, checklists,) or impossible (How do I reach all those teachers, or how can I be an expert in every subject?). (Fullan, 2014, p.6)

Consequently, in order to effectively lead in light of all the pressures and responsibilities inherent in high schools, developing capacity in others and then letting them take the reins is critical.

Structural: Does Your Administrative Structure Make Sense?

Structure impacts culture and vice versa. There are a variety of administrative structures that can be effective in schools, so we do not propose one that will work for everyone. Large high schools serving thousands of students may require different structures than smaller schools with 100 students, and large districts may have to operate differently than smaller ones. One superintendent may have a cadre of support in the form of assistant superintendents, directors, budget specialists, and curriculum coordinators, while another may be superintendent, principal, athletic director, and budget director all at the same time. Administrators need to examine their resources and determine what makes sense for each unique situation.

An examination of administrative structure can be a really difficult thing. Or, rather, examining and effectively *changing* the structure can be difficult. Changes are going to impact people's lives and livelihoods, so they come with real consequences. Changes even at a macro, district level can have dramatic effects on an individual school's culture, so a thorough review of the current structure, as well as any proposed structure, is in order. The following Living Narrative is an example from our experience.

Living Narrative

At our high school, department chairs served as the teacher-leaders of each content area. Each chair received additional pay in the form of an "increment" (a stipend that increased each year) and a period of released time to tend to department duties. They attended weekly meetings with building administration and reported back to their departments about any initiatives or upcoming events. Additionally, the chairs weighed in on hiring, ordered supplies, and advocated for their departments. They were evaluated as teachers, not as chairs, and because they were a part of the teacher's association, they did not conduct formal evaluations, nor could they have disciplinary conversations with teachers. These conditions were not created by the department chairs. As a group, they worked very hard to support both the teachers in their departments and their students; however, the structure they worked in was simply not effective. The reality was that our curriculum was not aligned, students at our middle schools received different educations based on where they went to school, and these irregularities were dramatically impacting the kind of academic rigor that could be achieved at the high school.

When the district superintendent retired and a new leader took over, the first thing he did was speak to every adminis-

trator in the district to get a sense of what the district reality was. As part of that first year, the new district administration conducted an audit of the entire district, taking a detailed look at each program, expenditure, curriculum, and anything else that might have an impact on student success. Part of the focus was on articulation between middle schools and the high school, and whether the current model was the appropriate avenue for improving our curriculum and ensuring our schools were having the impact on our students they needed to have. The conversation included very difficult discussions about whether another structure existed that would bring us closer to our goals.

Ultimately, a decision was made to eliminate the department chair position in favor of district-level Curriculum Coordinators, who would oversee programs at both the middle and high schools. Several rationales for the change were shared, including greater consistency in curriculum, better articulation, more instructional coaching, increased ability to conduct teacher evaluations, and cost savings. Additionally, the positions were seen as entry-level administrative positions and were thought to be an effective avenue for "growing our own" administrators who could then move into higher-level positions as they became available. From a high school perspective, significant gains in curricular coordination and articulations were counterbalanced by the loss of positions that some department chairs held for many, many years. Teachers lamented the loss of people they could count on for support when dealing with difficult parents, ordering supplies, or addressing any of the other daily emergencies that might arise. Later, a dramatically scaled back "lead teacher" position was added to each department to try and address these concerns, but several years later, teachers continued to identify the loss of their department chairs as one of their top concerns.

The decision to eliminate the high school department chair came with a huge cultural cost. It came at a time when the high school administration was working really hard to build trust with a staff that had grown suspicious of administration, especially district administration. A positive culture is essential to success, and ours took a big hit. This was understandable. Several hard-working teacher leaders who were highly respected by the staff lost positions they had dedicated themselves to for years, and some would lose a significant amount of income as well because the most senior department chairs earned sizable stipends for their work. While the chairs were invited to interview for the new curriculum coordinator positions (and several did), the new salaries were not close to what their teaching positions brought.

Sometimes, school leaders are asked to do very difficult things. As the principal of a school just recovering from a negative culture, and as a novice in my role when the changes were announced, I was hesitant. I worried that the changes would destroy the fledgling trust I had built with the staff. I also knew intellectually that the current situation and structure simply was not working, and that the change would be good for our school in the long run. When the superintendent asked me for my support, I told him he had it, and that I would do everything I could to make it work.

My worries were justified in the short term, but in the long term, the structural change was absolutely the right thing to do. We did indeed take a hit culturally, but our staff was professional, and as we worked through the changes, we kept stressing the positive aspects of working with our feeder schools to more closely align our programs. The teachers put in the time and effort to work with the new curriculum coordinators on revising curriculum, articulating with the middle schools, making changes to their instructional practices, and continuing to support students. I am now proud to say that our four middle schools and the high school are on the same page. The curriculum at the middle schools has become guaranteed and viable, and the high school now receives students who are far more consistently prepared than they were in previous years. As a result, we have been able to make curricular changes at the high school level, resulting in tremendous and measurable student growth. This positive effect can be almost entirely attributed to a structural change that required coordination between district administration, building administrators, curriculum coordinators, and teachers. That simple structural change, while painful to implement, made all the difference in the world and allowed for changes in other areas.

Aligning the Pieces

The purpose of this chapter was to give you an opportunity to rethink your own leadership philosophies and structures and give examples to understand how to begin and persevere through the change necessary to reimagine your high school. While this chapter focused on structural efforts, Chapter 4 will provide examples of how to navigate the curricular lenses of change within your school. There are no hard and fast rules to how and where you begin, only that your process be logical, thoughtful, and impactful.

4 CURRICULUM: ADDRESSING THE ELEPHANT

*Educate and inform the
whole mass of the people...
they are the only sure
reliance for the preservation
of our liberty.*

- Thomas Jefferson

W e have identified four specific areas for schools to consider when re-imagining themselves: structure, curriculum, instruction, and culture. The previous chapter describes structural consid-erations related to the way a school is organized and the way its people interact with one another. This chapter takes a similar approach, but shifts from examining organizational factors to the meat and potatoes of educa-tion: where things get real and where students are directly affected. We are talking, of course, about curriculum.

Curriculum: What Are You Trying to Accomplish?

The structural changes to our leadership team described in the previous chapter's Living Narrative were not the only ones made as our high school and district reimagined what we were and what we intended to be. It is used as an example because it was one of the most important changes we made. Prior to adopting the new model, our curriculum was very poorly aligned with the goals we identified for ourselves. Largely grounded in ideas unsupported by current research and created in response to federal and state mandates related to graduation requirements, the goal was to create paths for students (usually based on their tested ability levels), allow them to earn credits, support students' graduation from high school, and help them move on to post-secondary opportunities. It is important to note that this curricular structure was created by good people with positive intentions and with the best interests of our students in mind. As our school demographics changed and more research pointed out the flaws in our approach, it became necessary to re-evaluate what we were doing.

As we reviewed our academic program, we realized it would never get us where we needed to go because it no longer matched our goals. While we certainly wanted all of our students to graduate, "getting them through" was no longer good enough. The goal for all of our students was, and still is, for them to have the opportunity to pursue any path they choose upon graduation. These paths may include community college, a 4-year university, the military, a trade, or the world of work. Overall, we want our students to have options, choices, and a real fighting chance to accomplish their career goals. Our curriculum, however, was based on simply getting students to successfully graduate. As is the case in many high schools, this goal manifested in a curriculum tracking system where students were placed in remedial classes in an effort to provide more support and develop basic skills. This approach makes sense on the surface. After all, if students struggle academically, it is only logical to provide them with some additional support and to slow things down, so they have more time to understand the content deeply. Makes sense, right? *Wrong*! There is little if any research pointing to tracking as having any benefit educationally, but plenty of studies showing it can have profound negative effects (Hattie, 2008; Oakes, 2005). Far from getting students caught up, tracking practically guarantees they will not experience the academic rigor needed to succeed.

The problem with tracking is that it assumes a student must learn information and skills in a linear fashion, and that each step must be mastered before moving on to the next (Rollins, 2014). The following Living Narrative describes this practice through the experiences of a student named Liam.

Living Narrative

Liam is a freshman who is behind on basic math skills. He is a hard-working student who is well-behaved, gets good grades, and is interested in school and learning. Based on a test score, Liam is placed in a remedial math class where he reviews basic skills like addition, subtraction, multiplication, and exponents. If the remedial level class is typical, these skills will be taught at an excruciatingly slow pace, through uninteresting and unchallenging mediums (e.g., worksheets), and with little opportunity to apply the knowledge in any kind of meaningful way. The class will be taught by a young teacher, as in most schools the most experienced instructors teach higher-level classes. In a best case scenario, Liam will actually learn the basic skills; in a worst case, he will become bored and tune out. Even under the best of circumstances, he will continue to lag behind. Why? Because while Liam is re-learning how to multiply and divide, his classmates in a "regular" class are learning Algebra, solving quadratic equations, and applying their math skills to real-world problems.

Fast forward to sophomore year. Liam passed his remedial math class with an "A." His reward? He is placed in remedial Algebra, where he again studies hard and earns an "A" grade. The next course in the sequence? You guessed it... remedial Geometry. Senior year, while his peers are studying higher-level math and preparing themselves for college, if he takes math at all, Liam will probably take something called "Business Math" or "Consumer Math." Liam, who still works fairly hard and is a very smart student, knows that "Business Math" is code for "Math for Students who Aren't All That Bright," and he understands—because he has been taught it many times—that he is just not all that bright.

Unfortunately, there is a snowball effect associated with this scenario. Because of a recommendation by an eighth grade teacher, Liam was placed in a "regular" level science class (Biology), even though his test scores were below the cut-line. Liam loves science and has been fascinated by all things scientific since he was very young. He passes Biology with a "B" and looks forward to taking more science classes. The second course in the science sequence at Liam's school is Chemistry. Although he got an "A" in his remedial math class freshman year, Liam's teachers and counselors believe that Liam's lack of Algebra experience will cause him to struggle in Chemistry. Even though he has good grades, works hard, and is interested in science, he is moved back a level in science (in his best interests, of course) because he is "behind" in math. Liam's new class comes complete with a title identifying it as a class for students who haven't quite made the grade, perhaps something like "Chemistry Studies." Liam gets an "A" in "Chem Studies," a class where actual experiments are rare, but worksheets certainly are not. Instead of forming hypotheses, observing chemical reactions and understanding the forces and properties behind them, his year is spent watching videos, making models of molecules out of drinking straws and Styrofoam balls, copying notes, and filling out worksheets. Always worksheets.

The third year in the cycle is Physics. Liam still loves science, and he is especially enamored by all things physical. He has a knack for understanding how things work and has been fascinated by gravity, attraction, speed, and other aspects of physics since he was very young. Liam subscribes to Discover magazine and devours shows like Cosmos and Nova. Ahh, but Physics requires math. We can't expect Liam to succeed when math is involved, so he is scheduled to take Practical Physics, where he, along with others like him, will do the occasional experiment (carefully planned out by the teacher, of course) and will mostly fill out...worksheets. At the end of the year, Liam's counselor asks him what science class he would like to take as a senior. Liam tells the counselor that he's not interested in science anymore and asks if he can have an early release instead.

As leaders review the academic programs at their schools, they may realize that honest efforts to help students by creating classes geared toward remediating their deficits and getting them through graduation have resulted in a lot of students like Liam. Simply put, tracked curriculums do not provide a rigorous education to all students and do not adequately prepare all of our students for post-secondary experiences. Far too many students are required to take remedial, non-credit bearing courses when they move on to college, costing them both time and money. Additionally, students in remedial college work are far less likely to complete a degree than those who enter on track (Chen, 2016) and an uncomfortable number more never attempt college at all. They simply do not see themselves as college and career ready because school has not prepared them as such. This is another function of a tracked curriculum. Invariably it leads to issues with self-efficacy (Hattie, 2012; Oakes, 2005).

Imagine you are a student like Liam. Every day, year after year, you see the same students in your classes, are stuck filling out endless worksheets, and are never challenged to really think. You never even get to experience learning with students who are motivated and on track, so you do not get an accurate picture of how exciting and fulfilling it can be. It is disheartening, especially considering that some districts begin putting students in tracks as early as fourth grade. For all practical purposes, this curricular structure determines a student's tenth grade science class when they are 9 years old.

Addressing the Elephant: Diverse Segregation

Academic tracking negatively impacts students of all types, but has particularly dire consequences when applied to minority and low-income students (Burris & Wellner, 2005). These students, who in many cases face greater challenges than their peers, fall further behind when placed in tracked programs (Ogbu, 1992). Even schools that celebrate their diversity can find themselves perpetuating a system of inequality. The following Living Narrative provides an example.

Living Narrative

The school community at a large high school is extremely proud of its student body and takes great pride in the way that diverse students come together to maintain traditions going back many generations. The city has always been a melting pot of cultures, with immigrants from all over the world settling in the area to work for the railroad, manufacturing, and heavy industry sprouting up in the mid nineteenth century, followed by a wave of new arrivals from Latin America shortly after the Mexican Revolution.

The town is traditionally progressive, coming out as strongly abolitionist prior to the Civil War and continuing to welcome refugees from all over the globe up to the present day. It is no surprise, then, that when school staff and community members talk about the school, they invariably talk about diversity as a major positive attribute in the school. People note that students from many different backgrounds can teach each other how to interact with those different from themselves in a positive and productive way.

When the new principal assumed her role, she was impressed with the student body, especially how considerate, polite, and hard-working they were as a whole. When she began visiting classrooms over her first few months on the job, however, something became very apparent. Her proudly diverse school, in that historically diverse city, where the community celebrated both the things that made them different, and those that brought them together, was essentially segregated.

In this scenario, no one was intentionally segregating students. There was no program in place ensuring minority students were placed in some classes and their white peers placed in others. The school was staffed by committed, caring, and hard-working professionals who would never stand for such a thing. Nevertheless, the problem existed. How did the principal know? If she walked into a room and the faces looking back at her were White, it was an honors- or AP-level class. If she saw a mix of races represented, the class was probably a more advanced class. If she walked into a class and saw most of the students were ethnically diverse, that class was invariably a "remedial" one. The principal repeated this process numerous times to see if she was overreacting or missing something. She wasn't. She was able to correctly name the level of the class in every single instance.

Similar scenarios may play out in schools across the country. Well-meaning professionals place students in classes according to defined criteria. This may include a student's perceived ability levels based on a combination of standardized test scores, grades, attendance, behavior, and the sometimes subjective recommendations of a teacher who may have to make similar recommendations for somewhere between 150 and 180 students. It's really no wonder that these processes end up placing a disproportionate number of minority students in lower-level classes. In fact, it is entirely predictable (Oakes, 2005). Tracked systems in diverse schools very commonly result in *de facto* segregation.

We have already shown that tracking can have dramatically negative effects on both student learning and on their self-concept. The effect is even more damaging when examined through the lens of minority student impacts. The most comprehensive examination of the effects of tracking students can be found in Jeannie Oakes' seminal work *Keeping Track: How Schools Structure Inequality,* where the author clearly identified characteristics of lower-track classes. These include the overrepresentation of minority and poor students, the lower level of quality instruction, the emphasis on rote learning, and even differences in the way students are treated by teachers. Students who languish in lower-level tracks begin to see themselves as academically inferior, incapable of doing high quality work, and less likely to identify themselves as pursuing post-secondary learning opportunities (Oakes, 2005).

Student self-efficacy, or lack of it, can have a profound impact on a student's entire life, so the last thing schools should do is perpetuate a system whereby students develop negative perceptions about themselves. Initially, administrative teams may be at a loss for how to equalize the playing field for all students. The simple truth is that tracking or "ability grouping" begins very early in students' careers, and they, the staff, and parents can grow very comfortable with it—despite there being no compelling research showing heterogeneous grouping having a positive effect on learning (Hattie, 2008; Oakes, 2005). Once we saw this inequitable system within our own high school, we knew we had to break this cycle. We also understood that detracking would be a huge and potentially culture-busting undertaking.

Our examination of the problem began with a review of what criteria were being used to place students in their classrooms during their freshman year. In our system, once students were placed in a lower track, it was almost impossible for that student to exit that track during the rest of their high school career. The process will seem familiar to most: students are tested in eighth grade, and their scores are placed in a database that included basic ranges of scores that qualify them for a variety of leveled classes. Next, middle school teachers provide recommendations. If the teacher likes a student and that student does their homework, the student might be recommended to a class slightly above what his test scores indicated. If a student is an attendance or discipline problem, the recommendation is almost always to a lower-level class. Counselors who help make placement decisions generally assign students to courses based on these recommendations.

Another hindrance in organizations can be the system for identifying students deemed ready to do honors-level work. The maze of gatekeeping mechanisms in place to ensure only the best and the brightest could access higher-level courses can be impressively complex. In our experience, parents wanting to appeal their child's placement had to first make a request to the counselor, who needed approval from the department chair, who needed to check with the administrator, who would then decide whether a change should be made. Additionally, no mechanism existed to identify and move students who had been misplaced early on in the school year. As a result, some students capable of at-grade-level or even honors-level work found themselves languishing in lower-level classes for a full semester or longer. Are you wondering what to do if this situation sounds similar to yours? Consider the following Living Narrative from the hypothetical River Bend High School.

Living Narrative

During the course of a school improvement review, the new principal of River Bend High School discovered a large percentage of students enrolled in low-level classes in core academic areas. For example, of the school's freshman class, 55 % were enrolled in a remedial math class, 47 % in a remedial Science class, and 40 % in a remedial English class. Remedial English carried the added requirement of a "Literacy" class in place of an elective. The principal noted that far more minority students were placed in these classes than could be justified by their percentage of the school population. He knew that these numbers were unacceptable, but he wasn't sure how to make the necessary changes without completely upsetting the cultural applecart. The staff had been through many administrative changes over the past few years and was not ready to fully trust him or his team quite yet. As a result, the school leadership team, in collaboration with department leaders, decided to implement the needed changes gradually and set targets and goals accordingly. Hoping to kill remedial courses through attrition, the team resolved to place no more than

25% of the incoming freshmen class into remedial courses for the upcoming school year.

Reports were run, and team members identified any student who had been placed in a remedial class due to test scores, but who had passed their classes in eighth grade with a "C" or better. Next, they identified students whose test scores indicated placement in a "regular" (i.e., non-remedial) track, but whose grades or teacher recommendations resulted in a lower placement. Invariably, these placements were due to factors unrelated to academic ability, such as discipline and attendance. The team decided to "bump up" all such students and place them in the academically appropriate class. Philosophically, the team believed that academic placement should not be compromised for non-academic issues. When all was said and done, significant progress was made, and during the first year, targets for student placement were met in English and Science. Initial concerns about students who were "bumped up" getting lost or failing in their new, more rigorous courses turned out to be unfounded. In fact, failure rates decreased. Based on these small successes, a similar process was used the following school year, with more students being moved out of lower-track classes and into regular-track ones.

In the previous narrative, the leadership team was feeling good about their progress. However, they knew the plight awaiting students whom their changes would not impact. They knew those students were more likely to take remedial college courses, and furthermore, they knew minority students were more likely to suffer that fate. It became clear that de-tracking all course offerings was necessary. Their question was how to do it.

The team began by sharing data with staff about the negative effects of tracking. The administrative team was surprised to find a majority of teachers welcomed the planned changes to the curriculum. This is not to say difficult questions were not asked. They were. A small number of teachers frankly did not believe in what was being proposed. They believed that de-tracking would hurt students because unprepared students would be more prone to failing the class. Additionally, their presence would require "dumbing down" the curriculum, which would negatively impact more academically prepared students. These were difficult conversations, but ultimately the plan was implemented, and de-tracking officially began at River Bend. Working collaboratively with department leaders and key teachers, the administrative team resolved to place all freshmen students in "regular"-level Biology and English courses the following year.

To say that freshman teachers of English and Biology had a rough start to the school year would be an understatement. They were suddenly faced with students who had never been challenged with rigorous coursework, and who had developed the self-esteem, work-ethic, and engagement challenges generally associated with low-track learners. Teachers had to adjust their instruction, incorporate strategies they had never used before, change their response to students who didn't "get it" the first time around, incorporate remediation and re-assessment practices, and simultaneously maintain the same high standards that they had previously held. After all, "dumbing down" the curriculum would defeat the whole purpose of the endeavor.

As that first semester progressed, a funny thing happened. Where the team expected to see more students struggle and fail as a result of being asked to do harder work, the failure rate went *down*. Where they expected to see classroom disruptions increase due to student frustration with higher expectations, disciplinary disruptions also went down. Many students who had never seen themselves capable of high-level academic work found themselves holding their own with their more traditionally accomplished peers. Best of all, students began to free themselves from the stigma of being seen as "slow" or less capable. Because the work of changing the paradigm of tracks within any high school can be daunting, Chapter 6 presents opportunities to rethink the role middle schools can play to help high schools begin to change the trends in tracking by sharing the contributions that middle schools can make to tackle this same problem.

You've De-Tracked: Now What?

One may consider that transforming a high school is more or less a matter of eliminating lower tracks. Although this step is helpful, true transformation is more nuanced and complex. In the following Living Narrative, the de-tracking experience at River Bend High School continues.

Living Narrative

In the first year of de-tracking at River Bend, a large part of the revised freshman course sequencing went surprisingly well. Students were accessing more challenging college and career readiness curriculum, there was less course-specific segregation, and freshman teachers were proud of the work they were doing. But a funny thing happened on the way to creating the next year's master schedule. As course recommendations began coming in, the administrative team realized a huge mistake had been made. They assumed teachers in newly de-tracked freshman courses would automatically recommend students for regular or honors-level sophomore courses. Consequently, they never officially eliminated the remedial ones. Unfortunately, a significant number of freshmen students, many of whom had earned passing grades in the more rigorous curriculum, were recommended for remedial sophomore courses. This was surprising and discouraging.

As the team delved deeper into why these recommendations were made, it became obvious that many were disconnected from academic performance. Instead, they reflected frustration with things like attendance, homework completion, and attitude. Placing students back in remedial courses after they successfully completed rigorous college-prep ones defeated the purpose of the entire initiative. The team resolved to change things. A series of events ensued that were predictable, culminating in an uncomfortable meeting with the entire staff, where the principal flatly shared the position that the entire curriculum would be de-tracked, not just the freshman level. While it is safe to say some of the staff were upset by this news, especially because they had not yet had to work with mixed ability groups of students, their issues were rooted in genuine regard for the students. Knowing that the concern was about student success, the administrative team harnessed this intrinsic motivation to better collaborate with the curricular teams.

Surprisingly, the teachers were not swayed by arguments about research, failure rates or anything else presented by school leaders. Rather, they were convinced by the testimonies

of their peers who had worked in de-tracked freshman class-
es and who witnessed student success firsthand. Sharing their
own experiences, teachers talked about how the change was
difficult but doable, and how they saw students grow dramat-
ically over time. The most impactful statement was made by
one of the special education teachers whose co-teaching as-
signment exposed his students to a college preparatory expe-
rience for the first time. The teacher talked about his own ex-
perience and about how the low expectations held for him as
a minority student could have left him with limited opportu-
nities. He went on to share the impact that he had seen on his
students as a result of de-tracking and how all teachers had a
duty to hold high expectations for all students. When he was
done speaking, there was simply no way anyone could contin-
ue holding the belief that tracking was best for the students at
River Bend High School.

Similar processes to the one described at River Bend High School have happened in many schools. When contemplating de-tracking as educators, we would certainly like to pull the metaphorical Band-Aid off and get it all done at once. It is likely that this approach would create such a significant amount of disruption and angst that a more systematic approach is the way to proceed. Once they have begun the de-tracking process, school leaders should then address each level as that first wave of de-tracked students prepares to enter it. For example, as the first year of freshmen de-tracked classes progress, sophomore curriculum teams should be working on de-tracking that level for the following year. As the students make their way through the sophomore curriculum, junior teams begin the process, followed by the senior-level teams. By approaching the process sequentially, teachers and curricular leaders have time to communicate, plan, reflect, learn from their mistakes, and ensure that resources and supports are available before implementation. This approach requires 4 years, but the end result is an entirely de-tracked program, with the added benefit of teacher buy-in.

 Each school situation is different and may require a unique approach. Take, for example, a high school trying to accommodate students entering from three or four different feeder middle schools. The process could then prove much more challenging. In addition to collaborating with the feeder schools on early articulation, high school leaders need to work hard to get skill deficient students accelerated so they can begin doing grade-level work. This is particularly difficult in math, so different structures may be needed outside of simple de-tracking. An example is systems where skill-deficient students are assigned to remedial Algebra and taught the regular Algebra curriculum over the course of 2 years. The problem with this approach is not completing Algebra by the end of freshman year means the student will never get caught up. An alternative course can be created that gives students the instructional support they need while still getting them through the whole Algebra curriculum in 1 year. For example, a school could create a regular-level course that meets for an extended period each day. Why is it so important to ensure the students are finished with Algebra after 1 year? Math skills are critical to higher-level science. By getting students caught up in Algebra, a school can allow the de-tracking process in Chemistry and Physics.

The impact tracking has on individual students is significant, but its effects on the whole school is perhaps more damaging. Be aware that the process of tracking is like a parasite insidiously attacking your school. To see if your institution is infected, begin asking some questions about students in remedial classes. Ask teachers to move away from worksheets and rote learning in favor of higher-level thinking skills. If teacher responses include phrases like, "I would, but these kids can't..." you know you have a problem.

The Other Elephant: Honors, AP, Dual Credit, and Other Advanced Coursework

De-tracking schools to eliminate lower-level courses is one side of the curricular coin, but it is not the only one. To be clear, when we talk about de-tracking schools, we are really talking about the elimination of remedial courses, not the elimination of honors courses. There is value in students taking college-level work in high school, and if we truly want all students to reach their full potential, schools should purposefully identify students who are capable of tackling an honors/AP/dual credit curriculum and find ways to schedule them into these courses. As we move students out of remedial courses into the at-grade-level courses, we also find ways to move more students from our "regular" classes into our college-level courses.

There are several benefits to this approach. One selling point is that families may save thousands of dollars in college tuition by enrolling in college credit-bearing courses while still in high school. Of perhaps more value is students' belief that they can achieve at high levels. Students who never saw themselves as college material may suddenly realize that they are capable of much more than they previously thought. In order to make this a reality, effort, planning, and support are required on the part of the school.

For example, when our school leadership team first began expanding Advanced Placement and dual credit offerings, we knew we wanted more students to participate, but we also understood this wouldn't happen in a vacuum. With our curricular teams, we analyzed data to identify students with higher ("A" and "B") grades in regular-level courses, and then individually invited them to attend a presentation about Advanced Placement courses. The presentation was open to all families, but we made sure to extend a personal invitation to students whose history suggested they could successfully make the academic transition to more complex curriculum. We introduced AP to students by explaining what AP is, informing them that enrolling in AP courses can impact college success, and sharing what kind of effort was required to be successful. We also expanded our AP offerings so more opportunities would be available to students in multiple areas of interest. To support students new to AP courses, our curricular teams created a 3-day AP Boot Camp course. This course supported students by introducing them to the academic realities of AP and teaching them study skills and strategies.

Just as it is common for minority students to be overrepresented in lower-level courses, they also tend to by underrepresented in higher-level ones. If your school is to be truly transformed, proactive measures should be in place to identify minority students who have demonstrated ability to challenge themselves, and then formally invite them to do so by enrolling in advanced coursework. This process can have transformative effects for students individually and your school as a community. To accomplish this transformation, teachers can be asked for names of students in regular-level classes that demonstrate the work ethic necessary to succeed at the AP or honors level. You will notice we asked for demonstrated *work ethic*, not test scores. Our belief is that students who are willing to put in the work will succeed. Counselors can discuss course options with students, and parents can be offered informational nights to discuss requirements and expectations. Additionally, our school pursued financing for students who could not afford to pay for the AP tests; we believe that no student should miss an opportunity solely because of finances. The reactions students have when they are told they can be honors students ranges from disbelief, incredulity, and thankfulness. These reactions are priceless, as is the pride students show when they successfully complete an Advanced Placement course and then pass the test.

The guidance counselor is a key component of advancing your AP/honors program. Initially, some staff will need to shift away from more traditional perceptions regarding traits of honors students who "belong" in academically challenging classes. During transition meetings in our school with parents and students, one of the messages that is now consistently shared is that *every* student is capable of honors-level work in some subject during their high school career. It is not a matter of *if* they will take an advanced course, but *which* course they want to take. This approach sends the message to students that each and every one of them is expected to excel in curricular areas of their choosing.

As our school began to shift the paradigm of who was an honors student and who was not, it was apparent that some traditional gatekeeping mechanisms needed to be removed. To the consternation of some teachers, we did just that. To alleviate some of the discomfort, teachers were assured that administrators were not going to "get" them if the percentage of students passing the tests dipped. After a few years of work, however, our numbers of students taking advanced courses improved dramatically; almost one-third of our students are now enrolled in some type of college credit-bearing course. As predicted, the average score on AP tests did go down slightly, but the number of students taking and passing the tests to earn early college credit increased significantly.

Guaranteed and Viable Curriculum: An Essential Key to Success

Adjusting the rigor of curriculum has been a priority for the administrative team at our school. Even with the progress we had made toward increasing rigor across the board, the curriculum wasn't guaranteed and viable. We knew that a guaranteed and viable curriculum was prerequisite for any kind of meaningful, consistent academic growth (Marzano, 2003; 2005). A guaranteed curriculum identifies important concepts and skills that every student at a certain grade level, or in a specific class, is assured of covering, regardless of the teacher. Viability is assuring teachers have the time to teach everything required by the implemented curriculum. Here is the problem: Most states require far more standards be taught than are realistic, given time constraints inherent in a school year. The number of standards impact curriculum (Marzano, 2003) as curricular teams are tasked with identifying what is *most important* to teach (power standards) and what *would be nice* to teach. Once determined and written as curriculum, it is up to school leadership to hold teachers accountable for teaching the curriculum while maintaining their own identities as professionals. We would certainly never say that all English teachers have to teach students how to analyze complex characters in the same way, only that they need to teach students how to analyze complex characters in a way that meets the standards of the curriculum. The following Living Narrative illustrates some of the potential difficulties growing from a need for guaranteed and viable curriculum and the flexibility to provide teacher autonomy.

Living Narrative

Mr. G. is a social studies teacher who primarily teaches American History. He is a Civil War buff and feels that it is the most critical event in the history of our country. The American History Professional Learning Community (PLC) works with an established curriculum designed to teach history chronologically from the time period between the initial colonization of America through the 1990s. The group has established key standards to focus instruction, as well as some rough timelines so that common assessments can be compared and the PLC can discuss where to improve instruction.

The PLC arrangement works well, for the most part, but runs into trouble every year when it comes time to begin the Civil War unit. While the PLC sets aside 2 weeks for the unit, and then some additional time for covering reconstruction, Mr. G. spends 6 weeks on the topic. His students do reenactments, create dioramas of battles, debate slavery, and hold lengthy discussions about states' rights and how good people could support an evil cause.

Students learn everything they possibly can about the Civil War, and do well on all assessments until they get to those related to World War I, the Depression, and the Cold War.

These are topics that Mr. G. has little time to cover as he rushes through units to get through the curriculum.

As school leaders, we always struggle with maintaining a positive balance between "loose" and "tight" (DuFour & Fullan, 2013). School leaders need to be flexible enough to allow teachers to teach in ways they are comfortable, but tight enough to prevent teachers like Mr. G. from using unapproved curriculum. We all have worked with teachers who simply decide on their own what they will or will not teach. This is unacceptable. *What* you teach is not an option. The curriculum must be guaranteed. *How* you teach is a more flexible proposition and one teachers understand. Freedom is a wonderful thing in the classroom, and we are in no way suggesting professional educators assume the role of instructional robots. That would be no fun and would also be ineffective as it would provide no flexibility or opportunity for teachers to adjust based on student needs. On the other hand, leaders simply must have the ability to hold people accountable when necessary.

Curriculum is a delicate thing. In addition to determining what needs to be taught, teachers and school leaders have to make decisions regarding whether to go deeply into topics or whether to go broader. John Hattie's research suggests that a balance between depth and breadth, and between higher-order thinking and surface learning, has a significant impact on what students learn (Hattie, 2008). It is vital for students to think deeply about topics, but they cannot, for example, construct meaning from a difficult text without first understanding the requisite vocabulary. Here is where we sometimes struggle. Curricular teams need to teach the basics, but they also want students to engage in higher-level thinking, such as writing, arguing, debating, and discussing. Higher-level thinking like this takes time to teach and practice. In order to have a viable curriculum, any teacher would say they need more *time*. How can high school systems gain more time for this necessary work? The answer is to *let go* of some of the things and focus on what will have the most significant impact. Going deeper into the content will have a more positive effect than going broader (Schwartz et al., 2008), but doing so will require identifying unnecessary content—sometimes content that people really like to teach—and cutting it from the curriculum.

Does Your Curriculum Match Your Goals?

Curriculum must match your school's specific, explicit, and well-stated school goals. While goals have to fit with state and federal guidelines, they should also align with students' needs in your unique school situation. This will require you to resist the urge to buy into the latest trend and place less stock in standardized tests and more into what your students need.

A great example of this is the current emphasis on STEM education. STEM education has many benefits. Our school has robust STEM offerings, and more opportunities in STEM courses are being made available for all students. What we *resist* is the notion that STEM courses and careers are somehow more valuable than others, as well as the notion that the United States is somehow behind in these areas. We are not. What we are advocating for is creating well-rounded students who have opportunities to do what interests them and not be pigeon-holed into some bureaucrat's idea of what a good student looks like.

Yong Zhao has often wrote about the importance of developing individual student talents and interests. Zhao stressed that it is impossible and counter-productive to try and get all students to achieve the same outcomes at the same time (Zhao, 2014). It is not even a good idea to demand that all students learn the same fundamental skills, but students should focus on where their talents and interests lie. By placing all eggs to one or two "core" baskets, students may spend 12 years or more on an education that does not prepare them for a career that interests them or for which they do not have any aptitude (Zhao, 2012). In fact, according to Zhao, in times of change, skills that were once valuable can become worthless, and those that were once worthless become valuable.

At a conference, Zhao used the example of Rudolf the Red-nosed Reindeer to illustrate this point. The acceptable standard for reindeer noses was brown or black, so Rudolf was not meeting the standard. This resulted in an understandable level of frustration and loss of self-esteem—that is, until the paradigm shifted, the fog rolled in, and all of a sudden a red-nosed reindeer became a valuable commodity (Zhao, 2018 IASCD conference). This is, of course, a simple illustration, but it has parallels in the real world. How many switchboard operators, stokers, or elevator operators do you know? Probably none, because the world has left them behind. Similarly, our students will be left behind if we do not teach them to think, and if we do not develop their unique talents and abilities so they can adapt, overcome, and prosper when the world inevitably changes.

The national trend toward accountability following NCLB was a tragedy seeing vast numbers of programs in art and music cut in favor of more "core" classes. This short-sighted approach neglects the reality that creativity, problem-solving, and entrepreneurship are essential characteristics often developed in the art room, band room, or woodshop (Zhao, 2012). Your curriculum decisions should reflect this fact.

Aligning the Pieces

The process of revising curriculum can be lengthy and difficult, but it begins with some simple questions. Does the curriculum match your school goals? Are all students guaranteed to receive the same curriculum, regardless of what teacher they have? Is it realistic for teachers to teach the identified curriculum in the time allotted to them? Do all students have access to a rigorous and challenging program of study that will provide post-secondary options for them when they graduate? Once these questions are answered, school leaders can, in collaboration with their staff, come up with a systematic plan to identify and address any area where the answer was "no." Throughout this process, which may take several years, efforts should be made to collectively celebrate meaningful achievements and recognize both staff and students for the sometimes difficult work they are doing while keeping a laser focus on continuous improvement. After navigating the obstacles inherent in the journey, the school community will realize the satisfaction that comes with a job well done.

5 INSTRUCTION: WHERE THE RUBBER MEETS THE ROAD

*Education is not the
filling of a pot, but the
lighting of a fire.*

- W.B. Yeats

When cultural, structural, and curricular issues are stripped away, you are left with the essence of what your school is: teachers in a room teaching. In the long run, nothing is going to matter more than the relationships students have with those teachers and the teachers' approaches to their jobs (Hattie, 2009). Teaching is both an art and a science. It's a science because it requires expert practitioners to understand best practice and apply specific techniques to specific situations in order to achieve predetermined goals. They must develop an impressive array of research-based instructional strategies appropriate for visual, auditory, and physical learners. Like any scientist, they must develop protocols and methods on their own, and then test and compare their results with those of their peers to determine what works best. Teaching is an art because it is ever-changing. Each class is composed of multiple individual humans all keeping time with their own personal drum. Teachers have to understand in the moment how to adjust their methods and lessons to get the most out of each one. Like a landscape painter trying to capture a fleeting glint of light and color at sundown, a teacher tries to capture the wispy trails of wonder emanating from each student and then pull on those delicate strings in order to draw the students closer. There are few professions that combine the scientific and the artistic as seamlessly as teaching.

Instruction: What's Going on in the Classroom?

Like both science and art, effective instruction must come with some rules. Scientifically, mixing ammonia and bleach is a bad idea, so as educators, we don't do it in school. Artistically, we know that we cannot come up with a bright and colorful portrait by limiting our palette to only blacks and grays. There are things we know are instructionally effective, and practices that we know have a greater impact on learning than others. Conversely, there are teaching methods that we know are not effective and that should be discontinued. It is up to school leaders to identify which practices are non-negotiable and expected, and which will no longer be supported, all while leaving teachers with the professional discretion to adapt their methods to their own styles and classroom needs.

Curriculum and instruction are sometimes used interchangeably, but there is a clear distinction between the two. Basically, curriculum is *what* is taught, while instruction is *how* it is taught. Instruction also includes how student progress is assessed and how assessment is used to both improve learning and provide feedback to students. Plenty of researchers have delved into the effectiveness of specific teaching practices. John Hattie's research is a good place to start, such as his ranking of the impact of strategies based on meta-analysis of multiple studies (Hattie, 2008; 2016). Some of the strategies that Hattie indicated as most effective include:

- direct instruction,
- spaced practice,
- feedback,
- teaching metacognitive skills,
- teaching problem-solving skills,
- reciprocal teaching,
- mastery learning,
- concept mapping, and
- worked examples.

Marzano, among other things, emphasized the importance of providing clear learning targets (Marzano, 2007). Michael Schmoker stressed elevating the essentials, like purposeful close reading, writing, and formative assessment (Schmoker, 2018). Instructionally, there is no one strategy or approach that will immediately solve all of your problems, nor is there one area of research that is definitive. Schmoker, for example, claimed there is no evidence of differentiation having any positive effect (Schmoker, 2018), while Carol Ann Tomlinson, who has written extensively on the need for differentiation in the classroom, would beg to differ (Tomlinson, 1999).

Non-Negotiables

Ultimately, it will be up to school leaders to decide what instructional practices are to be stressed in your school, which are required in every classroom and which are no longer acceptable, but in order to get staff buy-in it is always a good idea to have a team (including teachers) gather research, identify what practices will have the greatest impact, share them with staff, and clearly explain why each should be implemented. For example, the non-negotiable of posting learning goals is supported by a lot of research. Perhaps the easiest to understand is John Hattie's concept of effect size and hinge points. According to his research, for a practice to be in the Zone of Desired Effects, its effect size should be greater than the "hinge point" of $d = 0.4$ (Hattie, 2008). According to Hattie, the effect size of posting learning objectives as opposed to not posting them is $d = 0.68$, which is well within the zone of desired effects. Similarly, teacher clarity, which includes making learning goals transparent to students, has a tremendously positive impact on learning in the $d = 0.75$ range (Hattie & Zierer, 2018).

These results are pretty clear that students do better when they understand both where they are in their learning journey and where they are expected to be when it ends. Providing learning objectives makes it easier for them to understand connections between learning activities as well make meaning of what they are doing (Marzano, 2003). For these reasons, at our high school, all teachers post learning objectives for each and every lesson. We also ask teachers to explicitly review these learning objectives with students, stress the need to assess the learning goals, and then have students self-assess their progress toward reaching them. Because sharing learning goals is a fairly easy task and has significant impact on student learning, implementing the practice in all classrooms is something that teachers can easily buy into.

Non-negotiable instructional practices (instructional practices required of teachers) can be sources of tension with staff members, and can come across as autocratic and "top-down" if they are not developed collaboratively. Teachers can and should be a part of the process and should ideally hold each other accountable for everyone implementing with fidelity. This is one of the few times where, in rare circumstances, a "top-down" approach might be required. For example, if an instructional practice is absolutely essential to learning, but teachers simply refuse to accept it, the administration may have to unilaterally make it a non-negotiable. To be clear, this scenario is rare and points to significant school culture issues that need addressing, but non-negotiables ultimately focus on what is good for the students, not what is best or most convenient for the adults. Your teachers will understand and accept this.

Because "non-negotiables" eventually become directives, and directives can come with baggage, the most important advice we can give is to *keep them to a minimum*! If a lengthy list of requirements is created, even if it is created in collaboration with teachers, it may be met with resistance. We suggest limiting these practices to the *most important things* that you know are *supported by research* and that can be *easily implemented* by staff.

Once you have identified a few key non-negotiable practices that teachers are required to implement, the next step is to decide what practices and teaching methods are being employed in your buildings that are counterproductive. This process should also be done in collaboration with teacher teams and be supported by research. When counterproductive practices are identified a clear message must be sent setting the expectation that they stop. This process may be a much tougher nut to crack, and has the potential for creating consternation and push-back on the part of some staff. The following fictitious side-by-side comparison of two Living Narratives provides varying perspectives on how to tackle eliminating negative instructional practices.

Living Narrative

At Prairie Path High School, administrative walkthrough and evaluation data show most teachers do not provided definitive closure for their lessons. In fact, during most classes students begin packing up their things and lining up at the door, usually with about two minutes left in the period.

The new principal, knowing that there is much curriculum to implement through engaging lessons, asks teachers to teach to the bell and eliminate lining up at the door. Though there is some initial ill-will (the teachers don't see 2 minutes at the end of a period as a big deal), the principal puts it in perspective by identifying how much time is actually being lost. Doing some simple math, she shares that 2 minutes per day, multiplied by 176 school days, equates to seven full class periods (50 minute periods) missed per year, per subject. If each student goes to a minimum of six classes per day, the result is 42 full periods of instruction lost per student, per year. Multiply this total by the student population, which is 1,000 students, and you arrive at 4,200 instructional hours sacrificed to students lining up at the door.

Her teachers, seeing the impact of the lost time, get on board and change their practices. Importantly, some time is set aside during a school improvement in-service day to discuss ways to use exit slips, provide guided practice, assess students informally, and otherwise use the recovered time productively.

Living Narrative

North City High School, a large school of 3,000 students, is located in an urban setting. As he is walking the halls and visiting classrooms informally, the veteran principal notices that, in many classrooms, students are watching full-length movies. Some are documentaries, some are Hollywood productions, and some are even episodes of popular TV programs. The principal knows there is a body of research pointing to short video clips as being effective pedagogical tools, but very little supporting the use of lengthy ones (Braeme, 2015).

He knows that he has to put a stop to the practice, as it is ineffective and consumes a tremendous amount of instructional time. He knows that there needs to be some direction on the use of video resources, but also that this direction must be nuanced. Realizing this, the principal decides to gather feedback in the form of a survey, as well as to bring together a group of teachers to discuss the issue.

Ultimately, the teacher committee decides to do some research on best practices, and they come up with some guidelines on the use of movies and videos in class. Their solution does include a non-negotiable, as the team believes that a rule prohibiting the showing of full-length movies is warranted. The teachers agree to develop teacher-driven professional development on how to effectively use video clips during instruction, rather than full movies.

After engaging in some professional development discussions, they realized that showing clips could be more effective than showing the entire movie, as short examples provided opportunities for discussion and reflection on the part of students.

With the help of his teacher leaders, the final task of the experienced principal was to provide an appeal process for teachers who felt so strongly about using a full-length visual text that they saw no other way to adequately cover the topic.

In these cases, the teachers were expected to provide a written rationale, and then bring it to their department chair. If the chair approved, the proposal went to the assistant principal for final approval. With this provision in place, teachers felt like their voices were heard and complied with the new rule. Many hours of effective instruction were recovered.

The principal at North City High is faced with a more difficult dilemma than his counterpart at Prairie Path. While it is easy to assume that teachers showing lengthy movies are simply looking for respite in their busy day, it is much more likely that the majority of teachers are well-intentioned and convinced that their use of movies is effective and an interesting way to get students connected to the material. Unlike the Prairie Path High example, where the principal knew that she would be mandating a change in practice, the principal here genuinely wanted to understand teachers' perspectives of the issue and then respond accordingly.

Everyday Instruction

While your non-negotiables are an essential component to be addressed in high schools, the other everyday instructional practices teachers engage in are of far greater importance. As we mentioned before, teachers need to be able to use the methods they are comfortable with. Some methods, however, are far more effective than others, and some practices are not very effective at all. If you want to re-imagine your high school, you will need to identify what practices are to be stressed and which should be discouraged. Unlike identifying non-negotiables, this process takes time. It also takes a consistent vision that doesn't change. Vision is very important here, because the goals you set for your school will drive your instructional practices. This step requires the authentic creation of a vision for success committing to the focus required for success as outlined in Chapter 2.

Perhaps the best way to illustrate what is meant here is to identify the instructional practices stressed in our high school. As mentioned earlier, the goal for all students is for them to have options when they graduate. We want them to be college and career ready, meaning that students are able to pursue whatever post-secondary course they set for themselves, and have the skills and background to succeed regardless of what they choose. This is a very broad goal. In order to reach it, our curricular teams identified what each student should be able to do, what abilities teachers would need, as well as the critical success factors.

As a school, we decided that first, students need to be able to think and solve problems. Regardless of where they end up, the need to gather information, interpret it, and then apply the knowledge to real-world situations is universal. The next thing that students will have to do is to communicate effectively. Jobs and careers exist where communication is more important than in others, but everyone needs to be able to make themselves understood and to clearly communicate their ideas. Finally, students need to have skills which allow them to function in both local, national, and global communities. This reality means that students will need to understand how to be informed citizens, how to differentiate good information from bad, and how to interact with other people as members of a civil society.

You will note that our broad goals for students do not include the ability to take tests or regurgitate information. We take standardized testing seriously and include growth measures on standardized tests in some of our short-term goal setting; however, testing does not drive our instruction. Here's why: as educators, we all understand schools will be judged in large part upon test scores, and we accept that fact. It is inevitable. We strongly believe, however, that if the focus is on shared goals and instructional strategies are implemented to bring them to fruition, test scores will take care of themselves.

Based on your own school goals, the next step is to determine which instructional practices will be stressed and which to de-emphasize. This task is more difficult than it first appears. As professionals, we like to read about what works and what does not. We attend conferences where experts tell us about the latest trends or teaching techniques. Vendors try to sell us curricula, interventions, measurement tools, resources, and social programs. It is important to understand all of these things. To ignore them would be to live in a state of ignorance. Consider what changes will make a difference in the long term. What instructional strategies will give you the most bang for the buck? Our school teams decided to focus our efforts in four specific areas:

1. Literacy
2. Questioning
3. Cooperative learning
4. Feedback

Each of these four areas tied directly to our long-term goals, and each represents a key aspect for student success after high school.

Literacy

Our first goal, literacy, encompasses both reading and writing. As a term, literacy is used globally to encompass just about any kind of program or initiative (cultural literacy, social-emotional literacy, etc.). That is not what we're talking about. Our literacy goal means that we want our students to be able to read and understand complex texts (both fiction and non-fiction), respond to what they read, make decisions on validity, form opinions, create arguments and support their opinions and arguments, both verbally and in written form. Literacy, quite frankly, is one of the absolutely essential skills for success (Schmoker, 2018).

To support our goal of building literacy skills, we determined that a review of our texts was in order. For example, the English department reviewed their curriculum, examined what was being read in each class, and asked difficult questions about validity, relevance, and accessibility. Once the review was completed, they made decisions about updating books, expanding student choice, and offering more non-Western options. The social studies and science teams engaged in similar processes. Social studies teachers, for example, decided that students' exploration of original texts was important. The department realized, however, that modern students struggle with reading some original texts, so in addition to determining which documents to bring in, they also contemplated and instituted new methods for teaching them. In fact, across all curricular areas, teachers endeavored to read more with their students. Close reading techniques were introduced; these included teaching vocabulary in advance to increase comprehension, active reading, annotation, and summarization. Additionally, students are consistently required to write about what they have read, summarize what they've learned, and participate in blogging, critiquing, and editing activities where they comment on claims, evidence, and reasoning in order to support their conclusions.

Questioning

Questioning is the primary vehicle through which students can achieve the goal of higher-order thinking. It is striking sometimes how much teachers struggle with questioning, and it is unclear why. We suspect that this is an area many that college methods courses do not deal with effectively, but the reality may be simpler. Teachers simply tend to revert to the questioning style they have experienced for their entire educational experience, which looks a little something like this:

1. Teacher asks a question.
2. Student raises her hand.
3. Teacher calls on the student who raised her hand.
4. Student answers.
5. Teacher determines whether the answer is right, and then provides an explanation for the correctness of the answer.

This is known as the Initiate-Respond-Evaluate model, and it is really good for teaching facts and other things requiring simple recall; however, it is very poor at garnering higher-order thinking (Cadzen, 2001). Of course, there are variations of this process. In our experience, the most common pattern happens when the teacher broadcasts a question to the class, the students respond chorally, or individual students provide responses. The teacher then weighs in on each student answer and provides the correct answer. To the untrained eye, a class being run this way can appear to be active and engaged, and the discussion may indeed be an interesting one. A closer look, though, will reveal something different. If an observer were to keep a participation chart showing the number and quality of responses for each student in the class, a couple of things will almost always be apparent: the teacher is having a great discussion...with five or six students out of the class of 32, and the teacher is doing more talking than the students.

Observers can track not only the number of questions each student answers, but also the quality of their responses. Use of symbols on a seating chart can be used to track single-word responses, one-sentence responses, multiple-sentence responses, and questions can be a very easy and practical way to share a wealth of information. When we have post-observation conversations with teachers, and we show them these participation charts, they often are amazed. Sometimes, they are a disconcerted. What they perceived as a very positive, engaging discussion may have been less effective than they first thought. For these reasons, we continuously work with staff on questioning, beginning with the elimination of broadcast questioning almost completely. Figure 5.1 is an example of a chart depicting the patterns of questioning in a classroom where a teacher relied on broadcast questioning.

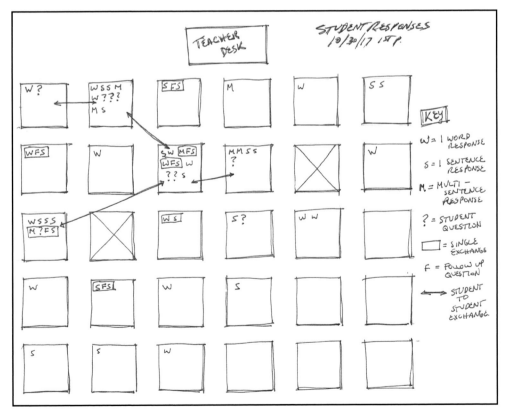

Figure 5.1: Student responses to broadcast questions.

Teachers initially struggle when we ask them to reduce and then eliminate the practice, and so do students. They may resist at first. After all, many of them are perfectly content to sit back and listen while their classmates do the heavy lifting. We warn teachers that this will happen and encourage them to persevere, paying particular attention to students who try to absolve themselves of responsibility by responding with, "I don't know." Once they've implemented and practiced direct questioning, teachers rarely want to go back. The increase in student engagement, reduction in off-task behavior, and decrease in behavioral incidents associated with this technique can be striking. Figure 5.2 shows the same class several months later after the teacher changed the seating arrangement and adopted a direct questioning style.

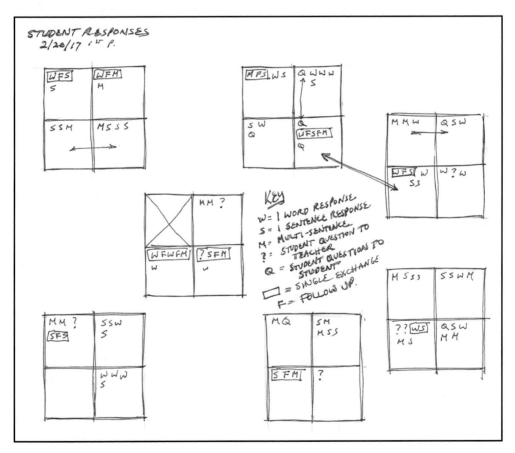

Figure 5.2: Student responses to direct questions.

In addition to focusing on how questions are asked, our administrative team consistently encourages teachers to go beyond simple recall or single path of inquiry questions (Danielson, 2009). Asking essential questions, or ones that promote higher-order thinking, is a task that requires planning, and teachers need to anticipate areas where students may struggle (Wiggins & McTighe, 2013). There is no expectation that every question a teacher asks is essential. Planning for that many questions would be impractical, and there is a legitimate need for recall questions as well. What we really look for is an environment where student thinking is being challenged, where students are questioning each other and where teachers are facilitating a discussion rather than weighing in on every single question. Nothing puts a damper on a potentially great discussion more than a teacher judging each student response. It is very difficult for teachers to step back and listen or to ask students to comment on each other's thinking rather than using simple compliments like "Good!" or "I agree!" Providing feedback to teachers, and offering specific ways to facilitate discussions, is key. Just as it is imperative for teachers to model what is expected of students, school leaders should provide some examples for their staffs. These don't need to be developed in a vacuum. A phrase lifted directly from *Making Thinking Visible* by Ron Ritchhart and Mark Church is one of the greatest questions a teacher can ask a student, and one we share with staff regularly: "What makes you think that?" (Ritchhart & Church, 2011) Staff members find this simple phrase to be one easily utilized, but effective in increasing student metacognition.

Cooperative Learning

Once students finally leave education for the real world, it is unlikely that they will ever have to take a high-stakes test again. (This is another reason it is silly that standardized tests drive so much educational policy). Students, however, will eventually have to navigate the imperfect world of human beings, each coming with their own unique quirks and personality traits. As a result, our goal, and the goal of any high school, should be to develop students who possess a strong work ethic, good communication skills, and the ability to work within a team. Herein lies another rhetoric trap: the public is constantly fed the idea that we are training students for some kind of global economy, and that students should be able to fit within that system like cogs in some massive machine. Our view is different. We believe that our students will need to think, innovate, and create a new reality for themselves—rather than fit into an outdated model of what an employee should be. In fact, we are not only interested in creating and training employees, although many of our students will certainly fill that role. Rather, we want to help students become leaders, entrepreneurs and employers that lead future generations. In order to realize this goal, students need opportunities to lead, discuss, process, innovate, debate, and work in tandem with others. One of the best ways to do this is through cooperative learning.

Cooperative learning, when handled correctly, can dramatically increase achievement and engagement, as well as help build the kinds of soft skills necessary to succeed in any post-secondary endeavor (Johnson, Johnson, & Stanne, 2000). Consequently, we have consistently stressed the need to include cooperative learning in all classrooms and have seen excellent results. Please note that we make a clear distinction between group work and cooperative learning. "Group work" implies students simply being put into groups and being told to get to work. Here is what group work generally looks like. The teacher shares an assignment, tells students to get in groups, and maybe gives a time constraint of some kind. Students, at least some of them, move to where their friends are sitting and begin working on the assignment. Most groups are dominated by one or two students, and there is usually a student or two that is (at best) a passive observer or (at worst) completely disconnected. Invariably, several students in the class choose to forgo groups altogether and work on their own. This is not exactly what we are looking for, but it is often what we get.

Cooperative learning is different from group work. It does not always mean working in groups of four. Some of the most effective strategies involve students working with a partner, for example. Successful cooperative learning requires structure, modeling, and clearly defined roles (Kagan, 1989; Slavin, 1996). We endeavored to reset the cooperative learning expectations with staff and began providing some more practical procedures with which to work. Teachers now are the ones to assign students to groups. Specific time frames are often shared, and students are assigned roles so that all are required to participate and add to the group's final result. This could be as group leader, timer, recorder, reporter, or whatever else is required by the assignment. Expectations for group activities are shared and modeled, with students practicing them and becoming more comfortable with them the more frequently they are used. When cooperative learning is done well, teachers will see an increase in engagement, discussion, and higher-order thinking (Johnson et al., 2000). Teachers using group work, on the other hand, will end up becoming frustrated and students will learn little. We know from experience that this is the case, because that is what happened in our school.

One of the great sins committed by educational leaders is that of assuming. Early in our tenure, the high school administrative team noticed that most classrooms were set up in rows of desks, with the teacher at the head of the class and assuming the role of "sage on the stage." Knowing this can be a very ineffective delivery model, our team began stressing the need for more collaboration. Drawing on our experience with cooperative learning in previous positions, we assumed teachers had the skills to successfully implement more cooperative learning in their classes. We were mistaken. Our teachers certainly had the will; many teachers began trying to put students in groups almost immediately. Where we failed them was in not providing any guidance, training, or support. The result was group work.

Feedback

The final instructional practice we decided to focus on was providing meaningful feedback to students and giving them the opportunity to self-assess. Formative assessment and immediate, relevant feedback allow students to understand their progress toward learning targets. Feedback also identifies what steps students need to take to achieve mastery. Many teachers have students track their own progress, so students understand how far they have come, even when faced with struggle or frustration. The effect of these practices has a significant impact on both learning and engagement (Marzano, 2003; Frey, Fisher, & Hattie, 2016).

Teachers can struggle giving feedback and often confuse assessment and feedback with grades. Many well-intentioned professionals still believe grades somehow motivate students despite significant evidence to the contrary. Some teachers continue to bribe students to do their best with points for success and zeros for failures. Some teachers suggest that they are holding students accountable by adopting these punitive measures, pointing to the "real world" when they do so. Fortunately, more teachers are buying into the notion that grades are a holdover from a time when we did not expect or want all students to succeed, that they were a sorting mechanism through which we identified students who were not cut out for school and were better off working in a trade or in a factory (Stiggins, 2004). Feedback, on the other hand, involves giving students the opportunity to identify where they went wrong, and, with some extra effort, recover. In *Seven Keys to Effective Feedback* (2012), Wiggins offers specific direction and examples of what feedback is and is not. Classroom teachers and school leaders alike can find specific direction and examples here to further enhance dialogue on this topic.

In order to be effective, feedback should be timely. We encourage teachers to engage in some kind of formative assessment of learning goals during every class. These could be thumbs-up/thumbs-down checks for understanding, exit slips, or short ungraded formative quizzes. More formal summative assessments are necessary as well, but when students do poorly on these, teachers should provide opportunities for remediation, as opposed to simply doling out failing grades. Assessment literacy is too dense a topic to tackle here, but educators need to ask themselves if it is truly important that students know and understand the material, or if it is acceptable for them to demonstrate they do not know, and then move on anyway. If the first precept is true, it becomes clear that allowing students to recover from poor performances is essential to learning. If the second is true, then we really do not believe all students can learn at high levels.

Once you have identified the teaching and assessment practices that you would like to see in your school, it is of utmost importance that the practices are stressed and reviewed, and teachers must be supported and trained. Teachers should have opportunities to work with each other, visit each other's classrooms and collaborate with one another. Leaders must be relentless in visiting classrooms informally so they understand what is actually happening. Teachers should be recognized for good instruction publically, and, if deficiencies are noted, these should be identified privately. Any time a problematic teaching practice is identified, the teacher should be provided some suggestions on how to improve. One thing we have found helpful is recording some simple data observed during walkthroughs and then sharing it with the teachers. For example, we may show a chart of improvements in the number of higher-order thinking questions observed or illustrate and increase in the number of observed cooperative learning activities.

Aligning the Pieces

Perhaps the most important thing school leaders should consider while reimaging their teaching practices is this: *keep it simple.* Nothing is more frustrating to a school staff than an attempt to start too many initiatives at once. Keep your big ideas consistent, your goals lofty, and resist bandwagon-jumping at all costs. What truly works in schools has not changed much, but it is easy to become lost in the vast wealth of information that is out there. Focus on simple, easy-to-implement changes that can be sustained over time; keep your students at the center and regularly communicate and celebrate your successes. Slowly, the ship will turn, and your school will be on its way to bigger and better things. All of this work may feel over-whelming in some respects. Chapter 6 provides insights in how to generate the capacity and energy to undertake the essential work laid out thus far.

6 CULTURE: WHY COLLECTIVE EFFICACY BEGINS AT THE TOP

*The thing always happens
that you really believe in;
and the belief in a thing
makes it happen.*

- Frank Lloyd Wright

Thus far, we have presented significant and challenging ways to rethink and reshape your high school through structures, curriculum, and instruction. The capacity, willpower, and energy to engage in and accomplish these changes are often in short supply. As educators, we are required to rise to the challenges inherent in a wide variety of teaching contexts while also living within prescribed time constraints. To do so, we desperately need resources to help us meet such demands. What if we had a resource that was not only limitless, but became more potent and abundant the more we used it? In education, that resource—while hard to create—is available. Collective teacher efficacy, or the collective belief of a staff in their ability to achieve the desired outcomes of the school, is currently the most impactful factor on student learning (Bandura, 1994; Hattie, 2016). It outweighs the income of a student's family, parental involvement, student motivation, and countless other factors (Donohoo, Hattie, & Eells, 2017). In other words, the collective efficacy—or culture—of a school is more impactful to students' learning than all of the life conditions that are uncontrollable and often lamented by school stakeholders across the country.

Schools with strong collective efficacy are places where staff members truly believe that all students can learn, and they are the ones best able to serve those students. These professionals persevere in the face of adversity; when they measure the challenges they face against their ability to succeed, they believe that their ability will win every time. Schools and teams with high levels of this construct are willing and eager to take on challenging goals, accept responsibility for improvement, and are confident that they will eventually succeed in any educational endeavor. The greatest feature of collective efficacy, however, is that it usually results in student success. In turn, that success creates *more* collective efficacy, resulting in more success, and on and on it goes. The cycle of results reinforcing effort is known as reciprocal causality (Bandura, 1977). This ever-renewing cycle makes collective teacher efficacy perhaps the perfect resource for any school. When schools possess collective efficacy, their accomplishments only increase their belief that they can transcend so many of the societal ills that people bemoan, but rarely present solutions to overcome (Goddard, Hoy, & Hoy, 2000). This construct is at the heart of vibrant, dynamic schools, the kind of schools we all want to work in and send our own children to. In other words, positive collective efficacy creates a positive **culture**!

At this point, we are sure you are asking, "If collective efficacy is so impactful and powerful, why doesn't every school just *do that*?" To be certain, collective teacher efficacy is elusive, and there is no magic button to push in order to inspire belief in self and others among a teaching staff. Collective efficacy is the by-product of many delicate and complex processes working in sync, the balance of which requires great skill and leadership to cultivate and maintain. This chapter is meant to guide readers through steps they can consider and questions they can ask, regardless of their role in any high school, in order to create a culture in which collective belief in staff can flourish to impact students' lives and teachers' well-being in sustainable and profound ways.

What Teachers Can Do

For decades, we have known that teachers play the most important and powerful role in students' educational achievement (Hattie, 2008; Sanders & Rivers, 1996). With great impact, however, comes a greater (and often unfair) level of responsibility. Certainly, we do not believe that teachers bear all the responsibility for the success or failure of students. In fact, we present strong arguments in the opening chapters of this book that unseen forces often create unrealistic headwinds that teachers must struggle against to do the work they have dedicated themselves to. Despite the hurdles presented to teachers, however, the tools and pathways are at their disposal to create much stronger counter forces to the challenges that they face every day in classrooms and schools across this country. It is the thoughtful use of these tools that can create high levels of collective efficacy, which, in turn, can create a robust learning culture for all students.

The Role of Standardized Tests

Standardized tests can have positive and negative effects on the efficacy beliefs of a school. It is critical for high school leaders and teachers to understand what to do and what not to do with standardized tests. Just as we advocated in Chapter 2 of this work, schools must define their own unique success, so it is imperative that teachers define worthwhile but realistic success for themselves and their students. Nationally standardized assessments geared toward college admissions, such as the Practice Scholastic Assessment Test (PSAT), Scholastic Assessment Test (SAT), or ACT, are not likely to yield timely or meaningful measurements of achievement, nor are they likely to inspire efficacy. These tests cover a broad range of subjects and the results take weeks to be returned. If a student does well, they often do not know *why* they did well. Was it their teacher's approach? Was it the prep course they paid to take in the evening (Schneider, 2017)? These tests do not provide informed feedback to teachers and students about how and in what ways their efforts resulted in achievement, and therefore do little to enforce anyone's efficacy beliefs.

Standardized assessments that are correlated directly to the course or courses a student takes and provide feedback on authentic test questions (i.e., long essays, information synthesis, and critical thinking) are more likely to impact student achievement and efficacy than multiple choice exams scored only by computers. Most high schools across the country administer Advanced Placement (AP) examinations every year. These exams are designed as opportunities for students to demonstrate their learning at the end of a rigorous course of study. The College Board, the administering body of these exams, not only provides feedback to the instructors on how students performed in relation to students in the entire country, but also regarding which specific areas of the content students excelled in or demonstrated deficits. Results such as these are excellent sources of information for teachers to access either as evidence of success or for specific areas of improvement. In either case, finding the opportunity to reflect upon such evidence of learning is critical to building efficacy beliefs within teachers. Leaders would be wise to create time and space for teachers of these courses to have both solitary and collaborative reflection time around this data.

The Role of Classroom-Level Data

When determining success in a high school setting, we advocate that teachers adopt a flexible definition based on context. For example, success for freshmen in an introductory English course will look different than it will for seniors studying advanced calculus. In both situations, it is essential for the teacher to internalize where those students are in their skill development and set challenging yet realistic goals for them based on the content and skills required in the course. Teachers should begin by providing exemplars of learning evidence and then help students set goals toward emulating those exemplars. Once goals are set, teachers can use the data gathered from classroom work (such as writing samples, self-reflections, or peer editing) to make determinations on instructional directions for individual students and even the whole class.

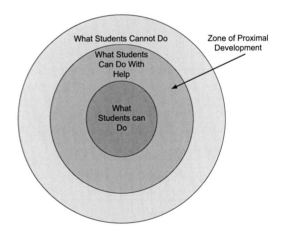

Teachers can also consider the work of Vygotsky and his Zone of Proximal Development when determining their instructional approach (Figure 6.1). In this representation, teachers are challenged to target students *above* their instructional level (the middle circle), but not so far above that they are lost (the outside circle). As we shared in Chapters 3 and 4, teachers must avoid living in the "easy" (the center circle), or they run the risk of creating an environment devoid of challenge, in which students stay at their same levels indefinitely. Such an outcome does nothing for teachers' efficacy beliefs or students' achievement.

Figure 6.1: Instructional approach based on Vygotsky's Zone of Proximal Development.

Another critical step for teachers is communicating rigorous goals early and often to the students, as well as communicating their progress toward those goals. Too often in high school classrooms, teachers surrender to content and pacing and allow the coverage of concepts and standards to be the only indicator of success. As a U.S. History teacher, I often used the period of history that I was able to cover as an indicator of my success for the year. If I was able to get to the Clinton administration, I considered the year to be a success. I would have had more impact had I concerned myself with the quality of learning that my students experienced, as evidenced by the work they produced, rather than how quickly I could get them to consume information. For every assignment, teachers must establish relevant indicators of quality that are aligned to purposeful course outcomes, and then work to ensure that their efforts support students in meeting those criteria.

One way to clearly convey learning outcomes is to begin a course of study with writing examples that illustrate the type of learning that students will be asked to demonstrate. This often-overlooked step is critical to achieving student buy-in of learning. Once goals have been made clear, it is essential to have a way to formatively gauge individual student progress toward that goal and communicate that progress to each student. One such strategy to consider is through writing rubrics.

For virtually every high school student across the country, clear and persuasive writing skills are critical outcomes for future relevance either in college or a career. Teachers can use rubric scores to have students identify an area of strength and an area of improvement in their writing. Students can then develop a plan in which they will leverage their strength and improve their area of need. Teachers can use the same rubric formatively to assess students' progress in their goals prior to using the rubric summatively.

When students are not successful, their teachers must use this as an opportunity for thoughtful reflection on how to alter their approach. More importantly, when students achieve their goals, teachers must take the opportunity to enjoy that success, examine how their actions helped elicit it and allow that experience to inform their own belief in their abilities (Nottingham, 2017).

The Role of Teacher Teams

Teaching can often feel like an isolated profession where instructors must sink or swim on their own. In high schools, administrators frequently create this dynamic by assigning the courses populated by students with the fewest requisite skills for academic success to the least experienced teachers, and then waiting to see if those teachers survive (Boyd et al., 2011). Over the years, this structure has created teachers who have become effective, yet independent practitioners on their own proverbial islands. The world of education has changed; no longer can our greatest challenges be overcome individually. The largest problems that are worthy of attention in education require collaborative teamwork sustained over years (Fullan, 2007). As educators, we must embrace this approach in both form and function. While an individual's competencies and strengths are important, they are not as important or as impactful as the competency and strength of the team to which they belong. It is essential for teachers to be productive team members and collaborators, not just isolated survivors.

Collective efficacy and the positive culture it creates can only occur when teachers are provided a forum in which shared beliefs, values and support can take shape. It is therefore essential for staff members to be open to collaboration with colleagues. Not only do teachers have to be willing to collaborate, but they "must demonstrate the discipline to collaborate about the right things" (Dufour, 2007, p. 1). It is easy to fall into the trap of focusing on factors beyond the control of instructors and blaming others for the difficulty of the tasks teachers face. While these pitfalls are understandable, it is essential for staff to maintain a focus on student evidence of learning, determining effective instructional practices as outlined in Chapter 4, and solving problems together is imperative so no one is forced into isolation. It is during this collaborative time when teachers create a shared sense of belief in one another and their collective impact. It is this collaborative time in which adults form productive relationships that the culture of the school takes shape. Without the willingness to participate fully and productively in collaborative meetings, collective efficacy—and the positive culture it fosters—will remain an elusive construct for any group of staff, regardless of the resources that they are afforded.

What Building Leaders Can Do

While teachers bear a tremendous amount of responsibility for student success, it is our belief that building leaders are not far removed in this shared responsibility. Within this text, we define building leaders as principals, assistant principals, deans of students, department chairs, team leaders, PLC leaders, and any other adult within a high school who takes on an official or unofficial leadership role. It is the job of these adults to ensure the work of teachers remains positive and productive. They are tasked with creating an environment that fosters the behaviors described in the previous section. Since collaborative time is so essential to creating the efficacy beliefs of a collective staff, it falls upon building leaders to ensure two things.

First, it is the job of leadership to ensure that regular, structured time is set aside for teachers to collaborate and identify best practices around a common curriculum (Schmoker, 2018). We do not advocate for any set frequency or structure to this time. Countless other giants in the field such as Dufour, Wormeli, Guskey, and Marzano have offered extensive research and recommendations on how to create and build such time. We simply suggest that by hook or by crook, high school leaders *must* carve out this time for staff.

Second, once this time is created, it is the essential role of building leaders to ensure that it is purposeful and productive. Simply putting teachers of like subjects together and assuming that productive collaboration will take place is irresponsible leadership. It is critical for leaders to remove hurdles for teachers, ensure they have access to data about their student's learning and have the skills to analyze student work and evidence of mastery. Most importantly, ensuring that teachers and teams have the trust and group dynamic to discuss data and instructional methodologies has proven to be impactful to student learning, regardless of ego or personal feelings.

This last portion, trust and positive group dynamics, is difficult to create. Our societal structures of government are built upon checks and balances which often serve as a replacement for trust. It is particularly challenging, therefore, for school leaders to create trust amongst teachers when trust is not systematically required in educational systems. To do so, leaders must take a humanistic approach which considers and accounts for the feelings and perspectives of all members in a group (Venables, 2018). The expectations and commitments of the group should be formalized early, and adherence must be frequently checked. It may even be necessary for groups to participate in trust-building exercises before true collaboration can take place. This may take the form of personality profiles giving team members insight into the thought processes and comfort levels of their colleagues. To focus on learning, you must first focus on people. At times, this may seem counterintuitive or too slow for ambitious administrators with a sense of urgency. But if true improvement and learning are the goals of a leader, then taking the time to create healthy and productive teams is essential and cannot be skipped.

School leaders are also tasked with identifying and communicating success and progress toward success. As outlined in Chapter 2, it is the job of school leaders to create a unique picture of success for any school and to communicate that vision to stakeholders. It is equally important for leaders to communicate how that unique success can manifest within teachers' classrooms, help teachers align their success to the goals of the school and know when and how to celebrate achievement of such goals. Leaders should be cautioned against celebrating superficial or unworthy pseudo-achievements; doing so risks diminishing the efficacy of their staff (Bandura, 1994). By recognizing and celebrating hard-fought and rigorous evidence of learning among staff, leaders are able to maintain a culture of high expectations and to create collective efficacy (Goddard et al., 2000). To do otherwise only embraces an acceptance of mediocrity without prioritizing hard-won growth and development.

The Role of the Principal

Thus far in this chapter, we have attempted to provide the importance of and a strategy for building collective teacher efficacy and a positive culture in any school. Collective teacher efficacy by definition is a social construct created by the interactions of a group of teachers. The conduct and beliefs of the leader of any group play a central role in the group's dynamic. It is essential, therefore that teachers' leaders (i.e., principals) possess and exude efficacy beliefs in themselves (Leithwood & Jantzi, 2008). It is difficult to imagine a school with high levels of collective teacher efficacy led by a principal with low levels of belief in his or her own ability to achieve the learning goals of the school.

With the centrality of the principal's efficacy in mind, there are two strategies that we recommend leaders employ to increase their own efficacy and that of their staff:

1. Have a non-evaluative network of peers to turn to for support, advice, and reflection.

2. Establish a school-wide focus through a system of continuous school improvement.

Non-Evaluative Peer Network

The role of the high school principal is a lonely and often stressful endeavor layered with unrealistic and daunting expectations. Often principals are expected to be experts in curriculum, instruction, operations, building management, labor law, athletics, crisis management, and countless other complex areas. Perhaps these unrealistic expectations explain why nearly one-third of principals are considering leaving their jobs (Markow & Pieters, 2012). Indeed, principals are confronted every day with the contradiction between the expectation that they must perform superhuman feats and the reality that they cannot do it all alone (Reeves, 2004). One tool that principals can employ to bridge the gap between expectation and reality is a strong network of non-evaluative peers to turn to for advice and support. Research shows that by having peers in similar job roles to access for support and advice, principals are able to hear about exemplars of performance from individuals that they identify with and can therefore emulate. Additionally, researchers have found that principals accessing peers for advice are less likely to make mistakes or strain relationships with their superiors, whom they are often less comfortable seeking out for fear of evaluative impact. Principals who regularly access a peer network show higher levels of self-efficacy in their roles and lead schools with higher-than-average levels of achievement growth (Dwyer, 2017). These peers serve a key function of reducing the isolation and burden principals may feel.

Principals would be well-advised to find and meet with peers in their school districts or surrounding districts whom they can have regular dialogue with on how to tackle challenging scenarios. In high schools, this can often take the form of others in a like geographical area, colleagues in the same professional organizations, and even fellow principals from district athletic conferences.

School-Wide Focus Through a Continuous Improvement Process

Success is present in some form in every high school in this country. What may be lacking is systematic success that exists directly because of the planned efforts and processes of a group of adults. This success—the kind that we are not surprised by because we intended for it to happen—is important to identify and replicate in your high school. Understanding not only *how* we are successful but *why* we are successful is essential in order to facilitate the student success that all educators desire. It is the job of the principal to design effective and collaborative systems of school improvement through which plans and areas of focus can be brought to fruition through the shared effort and ownership of as many people in the school as possible.

Creating and maintaining such systems of improvement is not easy and is therefore the subject of numerous works by massively accomplished researchers. Regardless of the size or makeup of your high school, it is essential for principals to be responsible for an improvement system that is sophisticated and flexible enough to address complex problems, yet simple and focused enough to enfranchise all school community stakeholders in a collective problem-solving framework. This system must give principals three critical assets: focus, the power of "no," and a clear process.

As mentioned throughout this text, focusing on a small number of initiatives and strategies is essential for any high school leader. With so many different subject areas and departments, most high schools can quickly become behemoth organizations with so many competing agendas that it becomes hard to keep track of priorities. By having a system of improvement focusing on a few key strategies, principals are able to coherently connect all of their school efforts to intentional outcomes targeting improved student learning (Schmoker, 2017). A focused improvement plan can also form the basis of every meeting, committee agenda and other commitment on a principal's plate. If a principal has a commitment that is a significant drain on time, they must take the time to ask themselves, "How does this tie into our improvement system?" If they cannot make that commitment part of the system, then they just found something that they may be able to give up.

The second asset is one of the most powerful words a principal has: *No.* Every principal leading a typical high school in America is inevitably inundated by countless products, proposals, and requests from people with "the answer" on how to fix their school. These could come from well-meaning staff members, school board officials, parents, district office administrators, booster club members, vendors and numerous others. As noted throughout this text, *there is no singular answer* to the challenges facing our high schools. It is essential for principals to play a central role in determining the select, yet critical, components that will be part of their school's plan for improvement. By arming themselves with the power to say *no*, principals are able to respectfully, yet emphatically, provide all well-intentioned people with an opinion of exactly how they can help. See below for a scripted example:

> *I appreciate your insight and your commitment to our school, but I have to tell you that we already have a plan in place and that (product/idea/initiative/book/curriculum/ course) isn't part of our focus. We are really committed to a few key things right now so that we can do what is best for our students. But since you are so engaged in our school, can I interest you in serving on one of our committees?*

Without the willingness to say no, school leaders will be powerless to stop the flow of well-intended but directionless initiatives. Once leaders say no to the things that don't support their vision, the focus and commitment needed to succeed may become a reality.

The third and final asset that a strong system of improvement provides principals is process. Even on the best of days, a high school principal can feel the job is daunting; on the worst of days, it can be downright impossible. When challenged by the complicated problems they face daily, it is essential for principals to have a process through which they can address difficult issues. When principals are faced with a task or problem to which they must find a solution, their job is immediately made easier if they do not have to also find a process from which a solution can be derived. By having a process that is clear and effective, principals can feel empowered to face all of the struggles they are tasked with addressing on a regular basis. But most importantly, a process of systematic improvement through which the work of the school is focused gives principals a forum to enlist the help and support of everyone interested in the success of the school. As Reeves (2004) noted, the job cannot be done by one person. Therefore, we encourage leaders to cast a wide net so that anyone who is willing and able to be part of the improvement of the school can find a role.

Impact

Building and sustaining a school with strong collective efficacy beliefs and a positive culture may seem daunting. We would contend that the building block of collective efficacy (i.e., student success) is abundantly available in schools. This Living Narrative about the experiences of a young teacher illustrates the positive impact that student achievement can have on teacher efficacy.

Living Narrative

Early in a young teacher's career, he had the enlightening experience of teaching an Advanced Placement (AP) course in U.S. History, as well as a remedial course in the same content area in a school of approximately 1,200 students, most of whom were low-income and came from minority backgrounds. In the AP course, the teacher had the pleasure of teaching Kelly, who was one of the most academically capable students he'd ever met. Both her parents were highly engaged in her academic and emotional development and responsive to inquiries on how to best challenge her. At the age of 16, she was well-read, insightful, critical, and engaged. She read the entire text well ahead of any assigned deadlines. She was able to critique the works that the class read with a clarity that many graduate students would envy, and her writing possessed an eloquence beyond that of most adults. By November of her senior year, she had gained early admittance to an Ivy League school and a variety of other elite universities.

In the same year, the teacher also taught Charles. Charles had no interaction with his father. His mother, while passionate and invested in Charles' development, had four other children to care for and often worked nights. Charles lived in a neighborhood known within the school community to be extremely dangerous, infested with drug dealers, and not safe to traverse after dark, or almost any time of day. A writing sample from Charles exhibited the uncertain consistency of an 8-year-old, with many grammatical and spelling errors.

Needless to say, Kelly and Charles were vastly different, but they had one key similarity: both were unafraid of hard work. In Kelly's case, she needed challenging texts and engaging writing activities. In Charles's case, the work was much more difficult. He had to be guided through reading tasks, asked questions in different ways, and demonstrated learning scaffolded over several assignments so he could work his way up to acceptable levels of writing for an eleventh grader. He needed a great deal of verbal and written feedback. Happily, they both graduated from high school. Kelly attended an Ivy League school, and Charles attended a junior college on an athletic scholarship before continuing onto a 4-year institution.

As the teacher reflected back on both students, he had varying emotions. He could remember how proud he was of Kelly. She was fierce, determined, brilliant, and driven, and is no doubt doing amazing things today. But if he is honest with himself, he already knew that she possessed those things well before she ever came to his class. If he is even more honest, he realized that she was going to find success with or without him. While her story made him proud of her, it did not make him any more or less proud of his teaching. It was Charles and his needs that made the teacher really stretch himself as an educator. When he saw the impact he'd had on Charles, it made him believe in his ability to change the life of a student who had the least but needed the most. Meeting Charles where he was and challenging and supporting him so he could be successful instilled in the teacher a confidence and energy that lasted well over a decade.

Aligning the Pieces

The culture of any school is the lubrication that makes all the gears work. Collective teacher efficacy is a profound and impactful resource that can create a culture that can fuel your work of rethinking the focus and makeup of your high school. It is also a delicate and difficult construct to understand and foster in any individual—let alone a complex and varied staff of professional educators. We encourage all educators to view all of their students like Charles as a path to efficacy. While students like Kelly also need strong and vibrant teachers, be sure to seek out and relish students whose success is so challenging and dependent on you that when they succeed they make you proud of *you*! Remember, the students who seem the most challenging at first are the ones who will instill in us the belief that we can do anything and change the life of anyone. Their success can cultivate a culture of possibility and hope in schools.

7
THE ROLE OF MIDDLE SCHOOL

*If everyone is moving
forward together, then
success takes care of itself.*

- Henry Ford

At this point, you may already be creating a mental or physical checklist of ideas, projects, or tasks that you want to begin in your high school. Before you get too far down the road, however, it is essential to consider the impact of middle schools on the success of any high school. This chapter is designed to elicit ideas and opportunities to begin the process of success well before students enter your high school as freshmen.

A recent work by Jim Knight began with some sobering statistics about American high schools: 1.2 million dropouts, less than one-third of eighth graders are proficient on the National Assessment of Educational Progress (NAEP), only half of high school graduates are ready for college-level math, and 14% of teachers leave at the end of their first year (Knight, 2011). These statistics are accurate, troubling, and in many respects, overwhelming. From the lens of a school leader or classroom teacher, such numbers create a sense of futility around efforts aimed at school improvement. Indeed, any individual or small group presented with such numbers will likely feel outmatched and dejected. The premise of this work, however, acknowledges the *individual* realities in high schools that *collectively* create the above statistics. Remember that no one school is situated to address these challenges on a macro scale. Our premise, therefore, is maintaining a focus on what can be done within a single high school, rather than fixating on the problems of an entire nation. If enough schools defy a trend, that trend will be reversed.

While maintaining a focus on a single school is certainly recommended from a strategic standpoint, we would be remiss if we did not acknowledge the important role that middle and other feeder schools play in the success of high schools. This chapter is dedicated to rethinking the ways that high schools articulate, align, and communicate with the schools where their future students spend the years subsequent to their arrival as ninth graders. For school districts that serve grades kindergarten through high school, the process of alignment and communication may be less complicated. In other districts, where the high schools and feeder schools are connected only by geography rather than similar calendars or district-level leadership philosophies, this is a harder proposition. Regardless of the bonds between a high school and its feeder middle schools, both are connected by a shared interest in the short- and long-term success of all students prior to, during, and after high school. This chapter illuminates avenues of change by proposing critical questions and ideas around educational transitions at all critical points of a student's school experience and offers guidance in two significant strategies:

- creating curricular cohesion between middle school and high school content areas
- leveraging meaningful supports to build academic preparedness and student belonging

These strategies and the subsequent tactics for alignment and execution are meant to provoke thought, discourse, and direction.

A Troubling Discovery

The following Living Narrative from Snowy Hill High School provides an example of a conundrum high schools may find themselves currently in. Consider the reaction and responses of the leadership team and the possible entry points to action that their story can provide you.

Living Narrative

*The leadership team at Snowy Hill High School discovered two troubling trends. First, many of their graduating seniors were placed into remedial college-level math. Second, upon entering ninth grade, nearly half of their students were placed into remedial high school math! This meant that students were taking **2** years to complete Algebra I, and they were not even being exposed to all the mathematical concepts found on the SAT and ACT tests until their senior year (well after the initial administration of these exams) at best. "No wonder these students weren't ready for college math!" they thought. They had created a system that practically guaranteed that students would enter college unprepared.*

The investigation did not stop there. Their next step involved asking, "What is happening that so many students are showing up to high school unprepared for math?" They found that in their district, students' path in mathematics was being determined before they even turned 10 years old. Students were grouped in fifth grade based on their standardized test scores from fourth grade. Those groupings determined which students would be placed in a math track leading to Algebra at the end of middle school (eighth grade) and which students would be placed in a math track that, more often than not, resulted in remedial ninth grade placement. While they were alarmed at these findings, they realized there was no malicious culprit behind the system. Rather, it was the result of years of well-intentioned actions taken in response to the needs of middle school students. Unfortunately these actions, while well-intended, were devoid of a guiding philosophy driven by clearly identified essential outcomes. While there was no one to blame, there was considerable work to be done.

The Snowy Hill High School team began by codifying and communicating the problem they had discovered to everyone in their system: administrators, teachers, families, school board, and the media. They juxtaposed this information with a bold solution. The answer required doubling of the amount of time students spent in math during sixth grade, rethinking the en-

tire math curriculum, adding more math teachers at the middle school level, a complete revamping of the elective structure of the middle schools, and lots of work between middle school and high school teachers and administrators. Needless to say, the work was exhausting, but it yielded great results. The standardized test scores of the middle school students rose considerably in 3 years; almost as many students are now placed in Algebra as eighth graders than not, and more students than ever are being exposed to Geometry prior to high school. This work had great impact on their entire school system and will continue to pay great dividends to the high school for years to come. None of it would have been possible without strong communication and the middle school and high school leaders working in concert toward a common goal.

The above narrative highlights that no high school can be successful without strong middle schools driving robust curricular expectations aligned with the outcomes of the high school(s) that their students will attend. The following sections offer a glimpse of how to create such connections in your school community.

Attack the Problem Head On

Numerous studies have been dedicated to the critical and delicate transitions that students make during their time in schools. Of particular note are the transitions from fifth-to-sixth grade and eighth-to-ninth grade, which involve moves to new schools (Akos & Galassi, 2004; Alspaugh, 2001; Dweck, 2014; McCallumore & Sparapani, 2010). Both of these critical junctures in education are usually met with dips in student achievement as the learners acclimate themselves to new social surroundings, as well as to new curricular and instructional expectations. What made the example of alignment in the Living Narrative possible was the way in which multiple schools came together to align under the same priority of college and career readiness.

We believe that the term *college and career readiness* is particularly powerful as a unifying push for contemporary schools. The skills and dispositions needed to be successful in college and the twenty-first century workplace have more overlap than ever before (Schmoker, 2018). By focusing on the skills that students need to have choices upon graduating from high school, schools are able to create a purpose that no one can dispute. High schools must work to leverage a cohesive purpose in order to align themselves and their feeder schools to achieve shared outcomes.

Again, consider the Living Narrative presented earlier in this chapter. The new leadership team asked their middle schools to align their course outcomes so that articulation into high school was more seamless and students were more prepared for the expectations they would encounter upon entering high school. What they did not realize was how grateful the middle schools in their district would be for that clarity. By offering strong guidance about where they wanted all incoming freshmen to be in terms of mathematical outcomes, the middle schools were able to leverage that vision to make significant changes to the curriculum, their instructional models, and ultimately the structure of the school day. In order to create the type of relationship necessary to make such substantive change across multiple middle schools, they had to first assess the status of their alignment. Like many high school and middle school relationships, the ties between their buildings were weak, and the transitions were more of an event than a process. The following section offers guidance on how to attack the eighth-to-ninth grade transition, create and align rigorous curriculum, and provide effective interventions for students in the years before they enter high school.

What is Your Transition?

Over the last decade, one point of consensus in education has been the critical role of ninth grade. Researchers have pointed to ninth grade as the year where students either establish the firm footing upon which future success will be built or where they fail to accrue sufficient credits, languish, and possibly drop out of school (McCallumore & Sparapani, 2010). Because the transition to high school is so critical, many high schools have implemented some form of transition between eighth and ninth grade. Transitions typically consist of counselors from the high school traveling to the various middle schools, sharing the list of the different courses the soon to be freshmen are eligible to take, and ultimately making course recommendations for the students based on a variety of data. The process is usually followed closely by an evening event when eighth grade students and their parents visit the high school, hear messages about the different courses, learn about experiences the students will have, and walk the halls that they will populate in the fall. Add in an occasional pizza party, class t-shirt, and maybe even a freshmen-only day prior to the first day of school, and you have got yourself the brand new Class of 20-Something. While these events are critical to help establish a sense of belonging and to create communication avenues, they certainly leave a lot to be desired.

Numerous scholars have found that students who struggle in ninth grade do so because they are ill-prepared academically for the rigors of high school credit-bearing courses (Akos & Galassi, 2004; Butts & Cruzeiro, 2005; Cauley & Jovanovich, 2006; J. B. Smith, 2001; J. S. Smith, 2006). As we all know, failing high school courses entails the cost of repeating courses. Researchers have posited that students who struggle most in high school English and math courses require earlier exposure to grade-appropriate content in order to prepare them for the rigors and challenges of the next level. This reality presents an incredible opportunity for high schools to create productive bonds with their middle school counterparts in two specific areas: rigorous curriculum and purposeful supports.

Area 1: Rigorous Curriculum

No company, team, or organization of any kind will be successful if all of its members or employees are immersed in a training program where expectations are low in preparation for a job where expectations are very high. Joining a new team with a different and more rigorous set of rules is a shock to the system. The same holds true for high school students. A high school that believes in and creates a rigorous and productive curriculum for students will not be wholly successful if the students transitioning in every year are ill-prepared for the next level. Unless the high school takes an active role in aligning and influencing the curriculum prior to ninth grade, they will contend with students who do not possess necessary academic habits, languish in the system, and eventually drop out or seek less rigorous avenues of diploma attainment. Just as the best companies, law firms, and corporations establish relationships with colleges and graduate programs known to produce high-quality candidates, high schools must establish relationships with their feeder middle schools in order for middle schools to produce students with the requisite skills to succeed in high school and beyond.

The first step is offering curricular coherence between middle and high school. By transparently sharing information and effectively communicating with the middle grade schools within their geographic boundaries, high schools afford middle schools the opportunity to align their curricular outcomes with high school expectations. This should happen in all content areas, not just reading and math. Table 7.1 presents some critical questions for high school leaders to consider regarding curricular alignment with feeder schools.

Table 7.1: Critical Questions for Curricular Alignment

Type of Question	Question Examples
Purpose Questions	What is the purpose of each content area in the education of students?
	Do *all* of the courses in this content area align to this purpose? If so, how?
	When considering the series of courses students will take in a given content area, what requisite skills or abilities would students ideally have prior to beginning that series?
Process Questions	Do the middle schools know what these skills are? If so, how do they know?
	If they do not know, who should tell them and when?
Outcome Question	If students don't have those skills prior to beginning those courses, what happens to those students?

After asking and reflecting upon responses to these questions, high school staff must decide how to proceed.

Although sharing the curricular starting points of freshman classes with middle schools is a good first step, more is likely needed. High school leaders may need to create supportive relationships designed to help middle school personnel create, deliver, and refine effective curriculum. A 2002 study found that only slightly more than one-third of middle school teachers perceived that it was their responsibility to prepare their students for college preparatory classes in high school (Cooney & Bottoms, 2002). Not surprisingly, another study found that the largest concern of high school teachers about entering freshmen was a lack of curricular rigor in middle school (Akos & Galassi, 2004). These opposing perspectives can, at times, make the process of curricular alignment tense and fraught with difficulty. By establishing productive, trusting relationships and strong common bonds with feeder schools, high school leaders can ensure curricular cohesion in order to the transition of students from eighth to ninth grade, while optimizing their chances for high school success (McCallumore & Sparapani, 2010; Smith, 2001). While the work of creating cohesion across multiple schools and grade levels may seem daunting, it is necessary to supporting student success and giving high schools a running start on improving student achievement.

In today's educational environment, curricular alignment is aided by the adoption of common standards by most states. Starting from universal, foundational standards, the process is aided by common language and nomenclature. In our experience, curricular alignment and coherence has been best accomplished by working with middle school leaders and staff to align capstone courses in various content areas for placement in high school. Table 7.2 provides possible ways to create alignment in various content areas.

Table 7.2: Areas of Opportunity for Middle School to High School Curricular Alignment

Content Area	Opportunities for Alignment
Math	Offer Algebra and Geometry courses in middle school so students can gain either transcript credit toward high school graduation or be placed in higher mathematical classes at the start of ninth grade.
English	Create and use common writing frameworks that are introduced in middle school and increase in complexity throughout high school.
	Create and implement common rubrics from sixth to twelfth grade so student growth in writing can be observed and feedback can take familiar and consumable forms for students.
	Develop and maintain writing portfolios from sixth to twelfth grade, so students are able to monitor their own progress.
Social Studies	Align curriculum to allow different course teams to eliminate redundancy of certain eras in history.
	Focus more completely upon rigorous writing and literacy goals within the content.

Science	Adopt similar safety and lab procedures so valuable classroom time does not have to be devoted to the same processes every year and more time can be dedicated to scientific inquiry
	Introduce certain phenomena prior to ninth grade so staff can leverage familiarity with a concept in order to explore deeper underlying concepts.
Career and Technical Education	Offer introductory engineering courses in middle school, so students can get a head start on pre-engineering courses prior to high school courses around design and modeling.
	Align career exploration around the Perkins Career Clusters beginning in sixth grade and throughout high school.
	Focus middle school technology education on the skills high schools have identified as central in grades 9-12.

Note: Alignment can also be gained through technological and/or social-emotional standards that bridge all content areas.

As you read this, you may be thinking, "That sounds great, but when would we find the time to do this?" We couldn't agree more; lack of time is a considerable barrier to authentic alignment. We suggest first working with feeder schools to communize the professional development days in your calendar, ensuring that teachers are available—without students or the need for substitute teachers—at least a few times per year. These professional development days may be used for leading productive dialogue around aligned curriculum.

Second, consider working with middle schools to target specific teachers to visit the high school, sit in high school courses, and observe what will be expected of their current students when they become ninth graders. Middle school teachers who see a high school class in action often walk away with concrete examples of how to adjust their own instruction, better understand how to prepare their students for the next level and witness new and different pedagogical techniques. By investing in these two approaches, it will not take long to determine the areas of curricular overlap, deficit, and alignment. With a skill and content gap analysis in hand, high school and middle school leaders can turn their attention to areas of potential alignment within the curricular areas outlined in Table 7.2.

The process of alignment will—and should—look different for every school. No matter the process used to create alignment, the creation of a shared purpose focused on the betterment of students benefits both organizations. All stakeholders will be pleased with clear and guiding principles through which meaningful impact can be realized and sensible contributions can be appreciated. Furthermore, clear guidelines and shared values help schools avoid disastrous, unintended consequences, such as the ones highlighted in the Living Narrative of this chapter.

Area 2: Purposeful Supports

A study on middle-to-high school transitions found that by examining sixth grade reading and math grades, as well as student attendance, it was possible to accurately identify 75% of the students who would eventually drop out of high school (Neild, Balfanz & Herzog, 2007). If any high school could be given a list of names and told that three-quarters of the students on it would drop out of school within 5 years, there isn't a principal on this planet who would not begin to intensively intervene with those students. Doing so, however, requires an understanding that success in ninth grade begins long before the end of eighth grade, and that strong communication with the middle school is needed. In light of the findings of Neild et al. and the centrality of the ninth grade year, it is of utmost importance that high school leaders not wait until the spring before freshman year to begin gathering information and understanding around soon-to-be freshmen.

Interim Learning

Strong and purposeful interventions intended to bolster high school readiness and a sense of belonging in an academic setting are critical for at-risk students (Dweck, 2014), and high schools have opportunities to create them. The first comes in the form of interim learning opportunities; for traditional schools, this time can be found in the summer months when the regular school year is not in session. For other structures, time may be found in other pockets. Leaders that are serious about changing the way students enter and experience high school must begin the transition to such academic expectations early in a student's schooling. By identifying the students most in need of intervention (as identified in Nield et al., 2007) and focusing on exposure to academic rigor more than learning deficits, high schools can help mitigate poor foundational academic skills, weak study habits, and a lack of perseverance displayed by students with a propensity for dropping out of high school. Schools can consider interim "camp" for at-risk students identified at the middle school level in an effort to engage them, teach them academic expectations and study skills, create a sense of connection and belonging to their school, and generally prepare them for life as ninth graders. Such experiences could begin as early as the completion of sixth grade and could ideally spiral and scaffold so students could have the experience for multiple years. Before worrying that attendance in such programs for students who already struggle to attend school during the regular session will be challenging, we would remind you to consider the age group. These are pre-adolescent children whose parents may have tenuous child care systems. Regular, adult-supervised activities with the intent of re-engaging students in school may be highly valued by the families of many struggling students.

Obviously, the cost of running such a program may initially seem prohibitive; however, we would encourage you to consider the high cost of students who repeat high school courses multiple times, require intensive administrative support, demand time from student services personnel, sit in online credit recovery programs for months, and (in some cases) *still* do not graduate. If there were an upfront investment a school could make in those students at a formative life point that could save all of the above cost and struggle, wouldn't it be worth it?

Fortunately, strong models for such work already exist. The University of Texas has created intensive curricula with supports to build positive mindsets around mathematics through summer introductory programming and school year curricular resources. This program simultaneously offers coherent curricula in mathematics and growth mindset that aim to enhance student efficacy and perseverance in this content. Perhaps of most value is the program's alignment from kindergarten through higher education (Blad, 2015). The supports and frameworks offered by this program, and others like it, can create cohesive bridges across multiple grade levels, with the intention of improved academic outcomes for students.

Create Belonging and Redefine Value

Another meaningful support high schools can create is a sense of belonging for new students. For some students, this will develop naturally through friends, siblings, athletics, clubs and numerous other traditional paths offered by most high schools. There are other students, however, who will not naturally feel connected to their high school and who will therefore persevere less in the face of adversity and be less likely to achieve success (Dweck, 2014). Approaches to this concern can vary greatly. An easy win can come in the form of yard or window signs given to every student prior to high school with the words, "Home of a proud future (insert mascot here)!" When students and their families see these in their neighborhoods, it can create a sense of school community and allows same-school students to make new peer connections early on. Another opportunity is to identify students at risk for low engagement in high school and begin a communication system between them and students who, despite having similar struggles or dispositions, have found success in high school. Such programs have been found to improve the academic perceptions and outcomes for African-American students on the verge of entering college; however, the findings have applicability to middle school students transitioning to high school as well (Aronson, Fried, & Good, 2002). The earlier that students can see themselves in the form of exemplar peers succeeding in school, the sooner they will be able to create their own vision for success.

High schools can also foster belonging by creating the opportunity for students to develop a new self-identity with scholarly achievements as a central tenant. For many students, elementary school was a period in which they were academically labeled (for better or worse) based upon their academic *potential*. High school is a period in which potential is less of a commodity than *achievement* (Oslington, 2018). By helping learners understand that the currency of high school is achievement, students can begin to understand that their accomplishments are more valuable than their previous labels. This builds learner efficacy more effectively than students simply being told they are smart or talented (Bandura, 1994). Leaders can create space for students to redefine their success based upon mastery experiences.

Aligning the Pieces

One fundamental truth that we have all learned in the face of numerous natural disasters in our country is that people want to help others. Time and time again, from hurricanes to wildfires to floods, our society has seen that people want to help others in varied and impactful ways. While the scope of devastation from a natural disaster initially appears overwhelming and insurmountable, it is the cumulative work of thousands of people working toward a common goal and purpose that brings hope, renewal, and recovery to those affected.

Similarly, we encourage high schools not to be overwhelmed by the scope of problems they confront, but instead to find a unifying purpose and vision for improvement and ask others to help. We hope that this chapter has provided guidance on how partnering with your middle schools can jump start the work of improvement long before students even enter the doors of your high school. Whether your path draws from these suggestions or you chart your own course, we hope you remember a quote by Edward Everett Hale: "No one can do everything, but everyone can do something" (1902). Find as many willing hands who can do something, and soon your challenges will seem like opportunities, not mountains.

8 A STUDENT BODY THAT PERSEVERES

> *It's not that I'm so smart,*
> *it's just that I stay with*
> *problems longer.*

— Albert Einstein

In order for a school to succeed, it has to develop students who can overcome obstacles, learn from mistakes, and persevere in the face of adversity. This is much easier said than done. One of the most difficult things for a school to face is students' perceptions of themselves. Many students walk through the doors of our schools believing that they are somehow incapable of succeeding, and this view of themselves as learners causes them to give up easily, fail to fully engage, or fail to try at all. Despite decades of effort to build students' self-esteem, the problem persists, and the uncomfortable truth is that it is partially of our own making. By tracking students, comparing test scores, penalizing them for not learning things at exactly the same pace as their peers, and creating a system where some students win and others lose, we have fostered an environment where the widespread belief is simply that some students are less capable than others. "These kids can't" becomes a familiar refrain, dooming certain students to a bleak, unfulfilling, and unhappy future. Sadly, no one believes the "These kids can't" myth more than the students themselves.

In his book *Overcoming the Achievement Gap*, Anthony Muhammad argued that much of the issue lies with our educational system being a meritocracy, or a system where talented individuals are identified, chosen, and moved ahead based on their achievements. According to Muhammad, our meritocratic system is responsible for the grading practices used in schools, academic tracking, norm-referenced tests, and even the accountability measures that many states use to rate and compare schools. The resulting competition is to blame for creating some of the pervasive inequities in the education system (Muhammad, 2015). Egalitarianism, on the other hand, stresses equality and advocates for the removal of inequalities among people (i.e., students). Only when equality is ensured can things like the achievement gap between the test scores of White and minority students be eliminated (Muhammad, 2015). Equality, of course, is something that we would like to guarantee for all students, but actually achieving this is difficult.

The issue of equality vs. equity has been debated in educational circles for many years, usually in the area of school finance. From a financial perspective, equality means that each student is guaranteed the same resources. For example, hypothetically, a state might decide that it costs $5,000 to educate a student for 1 year. The state then gives each school $5,000 for each student on their rolls, thereby claiming that educational opportunity is equal. Equity, on the other hand, focuses not on resources, but on opportunity. Some students come to school with more challenges than others. They may live in poverty, speak English as a separate language, or be challenged by disabilities requiring special education, so they are more expensive to educate. Seeking equity rather than equality, states like Illinois send more money to schools that have higher concentrations of these students (The Evidence-Based Funding for Student Success Act of 2017).

Equitable resources for all students is a laudable goal, but equitable resources do not ensure equal results. To guarantee all students achieve equally is a fool's errand, as there are just too many variables in a human population to do so; however, providing equitable access to rigorous, high-quality coursework, as well as the support structures necessary to help all students succeed, certainly gets us closer to that goal.

Providing equitable opportunities for disadvantaged students will necessitate that certain resources will be shifted, and that some classes previously available only to a select few will be opened to a wider cross-section of the student body. Some may wonder how these changes will impact students who are already high achievers, and they may struggle with the idea of a suddenly leveled playing field because high school education has become increasingly competitive in recent years. Perhaps it is due to the rhetoric surrounding the United States "winning" or "losing" the global race against other countries. Maybe it is because schools are now constantly graded and compared to one another. It could be due to the increased influence of companies geared toward getting students into the "best" college. Whatever the reason, the simple truth is that high school has become more about grades, points, and test scores than it should be. Why else would families pay thousands of dollars for test prep materials, courses, admissions coaches, and even illegal attempts to game the system by having others take tests for their children, falsify athletic accomplishments, and other nefarious deeds? (Page, 2019)

Some may perceive that the competitive nature of education isn't necessarily a bad thing. After all, students will need to function in the "real" world someday, and competition is something they will need to face, as well as the adversity that comes with it. When competition leads to a focus on grades and points at the expense of learning, however, it is not healthy. It is necessary for school leaders to decide how to handle it depending on the unique situation at each school. Many high schools have begun eliminating things like weighted grades, class rank, and valedictorian, citing them as emblematic of this unnecessarily competitive system. A growing number of colleges and universities have begun to reconsider the weight of these factors in admission decisions. Nevertheless, when changes like this are made, there is always a backlash. Here's an example.

Living Narrative

Several years ago, a suburban school district decided to phase out class rank, salutatorian, and valedictorian. Their reasoning was simple: too many students were choosing to forgo lunch and/or request physical education exemptions in order to take additional weighted courses as a means to inflate their grade point averages. Many of these students refused to take any class that did not come with a weighted grade out of fear that even an "A" grade in such as class would cause them to lose ground to their similarly-situated peers. The entire situation was unhealthy and resulted in students passing up coursework that interested them—such as art, music, or computer programming—to take classes in areas in which they had little interest. A gifted artist (and eventual valedictorian) for example, found herself taking AP Accounting, a subject she despised, rather than painting, an area of genuine interest and passion.

When the decision to eliminate class rank was shared with the public, a predictable outcry occurred. Families of high-achieving students spoke at several school board meetings lamenting the lack of support for their children. Most striking was the way that each comment framed the issue. To summarize, the majority of parents seemed to say, "My student is better than the other students, is smarter than the other students, works harder than the other students, and to eliminate the prize at the end of their educational journey will scar them for life." The decision was made to eliminate class rank anyway, and a surprising thing happened the following year: students continued to come to school and work hard, graduates were still accepted to prestigious universities, and nobody's life was ruined. Another outcome was that enrollment in art, music, and other elective courses rose. The number of students asking to skip lunch to have an overloaded schedule dropped to zero, and, after that first year, the issue never came up again.

This story underscores how competition has distorted the face of high school and how focused students and parents have become on "winning" the education game. The problem is, focusing on students' grade point averages and ranks can transform a school from an exciting and dynamic institution of learning where inquiry, questioning, debate, and learning are valued as ends in and of themselves into a bleak and joyless wasteland populated by anxious, grade-grubbing automatons interested only in the total number of points an assignment carries.

Creating an environment of winners and losers damages students at both the high and low ends of the academic spectrum. Students who struggle with school invariably feel as if there is no hope for them. With each worksheet or rote learning task they complete, struggling students become less invested in learning and more unmotivated. These students often adopt a fixed mindset, or a belief that forces beyond their control render them incapable of high-level tasks. We've all heard students (or ourselves) utter phrases like, "I'm not a math person" or similar expressions of self-deprecating helplessness. The effect of a competitive environment on the more academically-gifted student is equally dramatic, although more subtle. These students, who have always been told they are successful because they are smart or gifted, can also hold a fixed mindset, one that leaves them helpless and anxious the first time they do not meet with immediate success (Dweck, 2006). In both cases, students struggle with failure. On the one hand, it represents a self-fulfilling prophecy. On the other hand, failure represents the unthinkable and devastating destruction of a carefully crafted persona.

Accomplished educators know that failure and struggle are critical to success. This concept is foreign to some parents and even to a number of teachers, but failure is absolutely necessary if students are to reach their full potential as members of society. While it seems counterintuitive, the fact is, if you want students to succeed, it is absolutely essential that they be allowed to fail. The failure we're talking about here is not the "end of the road" of failure associated with a poor grade, but rather the kind where students see what mistakes they made and are given an opportunity to learn from them. When students are afraid to fail, they tend to avoid situations where they might struggle. As a result, when given a choice, they opt for an easy path instead of a challenging one. Unfortunately, the easy path is rarely where the most meaningful learning opportunities lie. In order to help students learn to embrace struggle, failure, and the effort it takes to succeed in the face of adversity, we must explicitly teach them that these things are an important part of the learning process (Nottingham, 2017).

What About Self-Esteem?

The emphasis on self-esteem in schools can be traced back to Nathaniel Brandon's 1969 book, *The Psychology of Self-Esteem.* Brandon identified self-esteem as key to success in life (Baskin, 2011). As a result, educators have been concerned about student self-esteem for decades. They worry that failure will damage students' self-concepts to the point where they begin seeing themselves as failures and, as a result, disconnect from school. For many years, teachers have been told that students' self-esteem is central to their achievement. As a result, educators believe that they should work to bolster it wherever possible. In the modern classroom, self-esteem boosting manifests in the form of compliments, encouragement, rewards, points, and students being consistently told how smart, pretty, or talented they are. Teachers are expected to help students develop positive self-images, and many schools have instituted programs designed to do the same.

As it turns out, the time, money, and energy invested in boosting student self-esteem has probably been wasted. In a 2003 comprehensive meta-analysis of self-esteem's role in success, researchers found the positive impacts of self-esteem to be overstated and cited programs designed to boost self-esteem in therapeutic or school settings to be ineffective (Baumeister et al., 2003). In the mid-1990s, author Alfie Kohn lamented the increase in curriculum being developed to help students think more positively about themselves after he found absolutely no support for the concept in the existing literature (Kohn, 1994). According to Kohn, Burmeister, and others, studies showing strong correlation between self-esteem and achievement were often poorly designed or otherwise flawed (Burmeister et al., 2003; Kohn, 1994).

The research, however, did not keep educators, social scientists, and parents from jumping on the self-esteem bandwagon. As is often the case when an attractive concept is widely shared but inadequately questioned, schools and teacher training programs rapidly adopted the building of student self-esteem as a panacea for improving student achievement. Teachers began telling students they were doing a good job—even when they were not. Drive-by compliments in the classroom became the norm as students' feelings became more important than hard work and mastery of content. During youth athletic events, every student received a trophy. The seductive notion was simple: If we can just help students feel good about themselves, the rest of the equation will take care of itself. Once given a healthy dose of positivity, students would suddenly invest in school, do their homework, think at a higher level, and transform themselves into the amazing intellectual heavyweights that we were consistently telling them they were.

Unfortunately, the foundation upon which the self-esteem movement was built was flimsy. Creating classrooms and schools populated by Stuart Smalley clones chanting, "I'm good enough, I'm smart enough, and doggone it, people like me" was never going to produce academic excellence. The movement included a fundamental flaw. While there may be a positive *correlation* between self-esteem and achievement, there is no evidence that high self-esteem *causes* academic success (Kohn, 1994). Here is an example that Kohn provided to illustrate this point: During colder months, many students come down with the flu. During the wintertime, people generally wear coats. Because there is a strong correlation between people wearing coats, and people coming down with the flu, coats must cause the flu (Kohn, 1994). Ridiculous, right? But this is exactly what proponents of self-esteem building initiatives have touted for years. On the contrary, research actually shows that efforts to bolster student self-esteem have *negative* impacts on self-efficacy, intrinsic motivation, perseverance, and interest in learning (Deci, Koestner, & Ryan, 1999; Dweck, 2006; Pink, 2009). These were not the effects we were looking for!

If programs designed to build self-esteem were ineffective, they could simply be relegated to the graveyard of failed initiatives, and we could move on while lamenting the time and money wasted on them. The concept that self-esteem drives success, however, has become so entwined in the national psyche that its removal represents a very difficult task. What is particularly disturbing—outside of the realization that something done for years is having the opposite effect we intended—is that the negative impacts of self-esteem bolstering strategies like praise and other rewards adversely impact things we value most, such as higher-order thinking and creativity, to name a few.

Thankfully, there is currently research being done in the area of self-esteem. Some of the most compelling findings point to rewards as being akin to punishments; a connection has been made because of their coercive nature. Learning becomes secondary to receiving rewards in the form of points, praise, grades, candy, etc. The result is diminished student motivation for learning, even in subjects students have a great deal of interest. As Daniel Pink explained in *Drive*: *The Surprising Truth About What Motivates Us*, "rewards can perform a weird sort of behavioral alchemy: They can transform an interesting task into a drudge. They can turn play into work. And by diminishing intrinsic motivation, they can send performance, creativity and even upstanding behavior toppling like dominoes" (Pink, 2009, p. 35). By offering students rewards for doing work, we minimize the importance of the work itself. After all, we wouldn't need to coerce students into doing things if they were actually worth doing, right?

Failing Toward Success

Self-esteem is not something that is conferred upon a person, but is rather the result of complex forces synergistically working upon a student over time. Rather than being built through praise and reward, self-esteem is increased through successfully navigating complex ideas and difficult tasks. In a nutshell, *success* creates higher self-esteem, not the other way around (Baumeister et al., 2003). Then why would we write about failure being critical to success? If success creates higher self-esteem, why would it be important for students to fail?

The simple truth is, in order to feel proud of an accomplishment and for it to be meaningful, there has to be effort involved. That is why the empty platitudes associated with the self-esteem movement mean little to students. A student receiving a trophy that he or she knows has not been earned means nothing to that student. These trinkets are often thrown in a closet and forgotten. Difficult, meaningful tasks that students can be proud of invariably require a lot of effort and a lot of risk-taking. The following Living Narrative provides an example from athletics to put this concept into perspective.

Living Narrative

Wrestling is a grueling sport that is both mentally and physically demanding. As athletes near the end of the season, they are beat up, tired, and sore. In this case, the wrestlers were nearing the end of a long, hard practice, and they were certainly not making their best effort. Drilling was sloppy, live sessions were lackluster, and there was a lack of energy in the room.

At a wrestling practice, an athlete was overheard complaining about what the coach was having students do for conditioning. When the coach brought the team together in the corner for a talk, the athletes expected to be dressed down for their performance. Instead, the coach talked about the reality of wrestling, how hard it was, how physically tough they had to be, and the importance of mental preparation to success. He even went so far as to point out that every wrestler, at some point during his career, dislikes wrestling.

He ended the speech with his most important point. "Gentlemen," he said, "This sport is hard. It's probably harder than most things you do in your life. That's why it matters. If it were easy, everyone would do it, and then it just wouldn't mean very much. When you win, all you get is your hand raised in the air, or maybe a little medal. But it's not the medal that matters, it's the knowledge that you earned that prize by going through all of the struggle and pain you're facing right now. You may never even win that little medal, but you will always have the pride of knowing you worked harder than anyone else and endured things most students in this school couldn't dream of enduring. It's the journey that matters, gentlemen! It's competing! It's getting up when you get knocked down. It's leaving the mat after a loss with your head held high because you gave it your all, and it's showing up at the next practice and doing it all again. That's what matters, gentlemen!"

The coach finished with a quote attributed to the man many consider the greatest American wrestler of all time, Dan Gable: "Gold medals aren't really made of gold. They're made of sweat, determination, and a hard-to-find-alloy called guts."

In this example, the coach pointed out that the process itself is worthwhile and the value of the activity lies in overcoming the adversity associated with it. He also acknowledged that participants would not be equally successful, and that some of them would fail. The coach described a growth mindset, or one where success is determined not by natural ability, but by determination, hard work, and learning from mistakes (Dweck, 2009). Learning in the classroom is no different. A person's mindset largely determines how they respond to failure, and how a person responds to failure is a key component in how they will fare in any endeavor they undertake. A student with a fixed mindset, or one who believes their success or failure is due to factors beyond their control (like natural ability), is much more likely to give up when faced with failure or may avoid any task where they might potentially fail (Dweck, 2016). Unfortunately, the focus on rewards and praise associated with the self-esteem movement can result in students adopting a fixed mindset, or one where the destination becomes more important than the journey.

It is stunning how many great people attribute their success to failure. Michael Jordan shared how failing to make his high school basketball team motivated him to practice harder. Thomas Edison made more than 1,000 attempts at the light bulb before discovering an approach that worked. The

Beatles and Elvis were told they weren't talented enough to make it in the music industry. Dan Gable, who never lost a wrestling match in high school or college, attributed his losing a single time to his development into one of the greatest wrestlers of all time. Entering the National Championship Tournament in 1970, Gable won 181 straight matches, pinning his opponents in 108 of those contests. During his final collegiate match, wrestling for a National Championship title against a sophomore from the University of Washington, the unthinkable happened: Dan Gable lost. He was understandably devastated, but then he made a decision: He would use the loss to motivate himself, learn from his mistakes, and become even better than he was before. Dan Gable went on to dominate international competition, winning gold medals at both the world and Olympic games. Wrestling against the best in the world in the 1972 Olympic Games in Munich, Gable was not only unbeaten, but no one scored a single point on him.

What all these greats have in common is that *they did not let failure beat them*. They learned from failure, worked harder, and persevered. They learned to "fail forward," as author John Maxwell described the process of turning mistakes into successes (Maxwell, 2007). In order to develop strong, resilient students, schools must abandon the practice of building students' self-esteem and instead build environments where it is safe for students to take risks, fail, learn, and grow.

Creating the Conditions for Perseverance

Creating a school culture where students persevere shouldn't be difficult. How hard can it be to get students to recognize that failure is not the end of the world, and that working hard to overcome adversity builds both competence and character? As it turns out, this is actually very difficult.

Self-esteem programs have been a part of schools for decades. They are embedded in the fabric of our educational institutions, and an entire generation was raised on them. Children raised during the self-esteem movement are now parents, and many feel that developing self-esteem in their children is absolutely necessary for success. As a result, many students come to us with fixed mindsets (Dweck, 2016). More importantly, high schools have traditionally been structured in ways that discourage risk-taking. Punitive grading scales, honors points, class ranks, academic tracking, and other factors all contribute to an environment where students are penalized for failing to achieve at the same pace as their peers. These structures provide little chance for recovery when mistakes are made. Our high school structures must change if high schools are to be transformed into ones where students persevere. The following are some suggestions for addressing these practices.

Teaching Mindset

Based on what we know about student mindsets and the impact they have on learning, schools should consider proactively teaching students how to recognize and adjust their own mindset in order to become more successful, both academically and socially. Recent researchers have found that students' beliefs about their ability to learn challenging academic material are malleable. In other words, students who possess fixed mindsets are capable of adopting more growth-oriented ones. The result of a growth-oriented mindset is better performance and more persistence. Fixed mindset perceptions are most common in math and science, so incorporating strategies to address them may make sense in these classes during middle school, the early years of high school, or as a separate support for students who need intervention due to poor performance (Lin-Siegler, Dweck, & Cohen, 2016).

In addition to targeting mindset prescriptively for students who need it, we believe that schools must develop a universal mindset message that is consistently communicated and instituted schoolwide. The message should be simple: *intelligence is not fixed.* Success depends on perseverance, effort, planning, and process. This message should be shared constantly in every class.

For example, imagine a sophomore English student is overheard quietly complaining that she is "dumb." In her own mind's eye, she believes this because she does not understand some of the passages in her assigned reading. The teacher overhears her and seizes the opportunity to use this instructional moment as a lesson for the class. The teacher does not identify the student, but calls the class together. The teacher draws a diagram showing a small circle sitting on a diagonal line on the board. The teacher tells the students the diagram represents intelligence (see Fig. 8.1). Students are asked to think about what the diagram looks like. One student offers that it looks like a ball on a hill. The teacher adds a new condition, telling the student that the circle was indeed a ball—a snowball—and that it is sitting on a snow-covered hill. He asks students to describe what happens next.

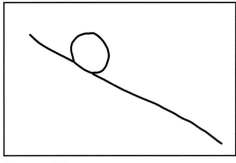
Figure 8.1

Predictably, students say that the ball would roll down the hill and get bigger as it kept rolling. Next, the teacher asks students to write a paragraph explaining how the snowball represents intelligence. Students are to share their paragraph with a partner and then share key ideas with the class.

The teacher calls on the student who is central in the situation. She shares the idea that just as the snowball gets bigger as it rolls down a snowy hill, intelligence grows as a result of studying, thinking, and solving problems. The teacher ends the short activity by stressing that no one in that room was "dumb" or incapable; rather, they just needed to roll down the hill a little further.

These are the kinds of messages students need to hear constantly: *Intelligence is not a fixed commodity.* Intelligence can be grown through hard work and perseverance. James Nottingham suggests that there is a "learning pit" that students must navigate in order to develop deeper understanding (Nottingham, 2017). In a learning pit scenario, teachers help students understand that the learning process is sometimes difficult, and show them the value in introducing concepts, creating cognitive conflict, constructing meaning by making links and connections as they deal with the conflict, and finally considering how they progressed from relatively simple ideas to more complex ones. Although this process is difficult at times, the challenge makes learning more interesting (and valuable) to students (Nottingham, 2017).

Grading and Its Effects on Perseverance

Talk is cheap, and words are not enough. People, including students, believe what you *do* far more than what you *say*. When we say failure can be an important part of learning, we have to be careful. When experienced in an environment where it can be used as a learning tool, failure is hugely beneficial. As a final result with no opportunity for recovery, failure can be debilitating (Kohn, 1994). Consequently, it's not enough to simply talk about students needing to make an effort and learn from failure, educators need to create environments where it is actually possible. If your school is one where learning from failure is only given lip service, students will continue to struggle. For example, if staff consistently talk to students about taking chances, pushing themselves, and learning from their mistakes, but then turn around and penalize them with poor grades and a strict "no-retake" policy when they don't do well, teachers and principals are only giving lip service to the concept. By creating an environment where re-assessment, revision, remediation, and recovery from first-time failure is possible, they are proving their beliefs through action.

If you truly want to change the learning environment for students, your grading policies must align with your goals. If your goals include actual student growth, higher-order thinking, self-reflection, goal-setting, and perseverance, a traditional grading system is not adequate.

There is probably no single area in education that gets teachers more fired up than questioning their grading policies, especially at the high school level. It's as if moving to anything other than a 100-point scale is a sacrilege so dire that fire and brimstone will rain down on the head of any teacher daring to question the sanctity of the system. Research on grades is not new; we've known for decades that traditional grading systems based on averages are inherently inaccurate. George Whipple in the preface to Isadore Finkelstein's monograph *The Marking System in Theory and Practice* wrote about the inaccuracy of grading practices way back in 1913:

> When we consider the practically universal use in all educational institutions of a system of marks, whether numbers or letters, to indicate scholastic attainment of the pupils or students in these institutions, and when we remember how very great stress is laid by teachers and pupils alike upon these marks as real measures or indicators of attainment, we can but be astonished at the blind faith that has been felt in the reliability of the marking system. School administrators have been using with confidence an absolutely uncalibrated instrument...What faults appear in the marking systems that we are now using, and how can these be avoided or minimized? (Finkelstein, 1913, p.1)

More recently, scholars like Rick Stiggins, Tom Guskey, Doug Reeves, and others have talked and written about the negative effects of using 100-point scales, averaging, zeros, and other common grading practices. Some teachers stubbornly cling to these outdated practices, and by doing so, create an environment where students are afraid to take risks because they know that the slightest mistake could have a significant cost.

Making the Argument

Changing grading practices in your school will be difficult. The best approach is to come well-armed with research, so you are ready to answer legitimate concerns as they arise. Remember, teachers generally want what is good for students, so if they resist changes to grading and assessment, it is likely that they truly believe their system works. You must be prepared with irrefutable data supporting the changes being advocated. For example, below are some of the most common arguments teachers make for using traditional grading systems, usually a 100-point scale with letter grades being assigned to specific percentages and averaged grades over time:

1. Grades motivate students to work harder. If I don't give a grade, students won't be motivated to do the work.

2. Giving students a zero for missing work will motivate them to turn their work in.

3. Taking points off for late work will ensure that students turn their work in on time.

4. In the real world, they will be held accountable for things like deadlines and submission of work. I'm teaching them responsibility.

5. A 100-point scale is a fair and accurate way to measure learning.

The five points listed here are all myths which have *absolutely no basis in research*, so when talking with teachers, be armed with the facts:

1. There is no evidence that grades motivate students in anything other than a superficial way. In fact, grades probably diminish students' interest in learning (Kohn, 1994; Stiggins, 1991).

2. Giving zeros (on a 100-point scale) is one of the most unfair and demotivating things that can be done to a student. It creates a disastrous circumstance that cannot be overcome, as it allows no opportunity for recovery. Zeroes also cause statistical sabotage, so a student's final grade in a course has no real connection to what they know or can do (Dueck, 2014). Students don't learn from getting zeros. They shut down as a result of them and may become angry and defiant (Reeves, 2011).

3. Taking points off for late work doesn't motivate students. This practice distorts a grade's ability to relay accurate information and actually discourages some students from doing the work (Dueck, 2014). Ask a teacher who assigns zeros or takes off points for late work whether their policy works. Do all their students turn their work in on time? Has their approach increased the amount of students turning in assignments, or do the same students still fall short? If they are being honest, they will admit that students continue to behave as they always have.

4. Grades are a very poor tool for teaching responsibility (Wormeli, 2006). When teachers play the "I'm teaching them responsibility" card, ask them if every staff member who turned in their grades late, missed a staff meeting, or came to class a few minute after the bell rang was fired or docked pay. After some uncomfortable squirming, they may realize that the real-world expectations they want to hold students accountable for are perhaps not as real as they thought. Additionally, the "real world" very rarely requires "one chance do-or-die scenarios" for demonstrating proficiency in any given field (Rshaid 2011, p.26). Pilots, accountants, and even teachers must pass a qualifying exam before assuming positions in their chosen fields, but rarely is success on the first try required. For example, the bar exam is a rigorous test that all law school graduates must pass before practicing law. In many states, it can be taken unlimited times with no penalty, while all other states allow multiple attempts (National Conference of Bar Examiners, 2019).

5. For those who insist that a 100-point scale is the way to go, provide more professional development. The 100-point scale was first used during World War I to sort thousands of soldiers quickly into jobs, and this system was not intended to measure achievement of a specific learning target (Marzano, 2006). The 100-point scale is inherently unfair because there are almost six times as many points in the "F" range as there are in any of the other categories. Provide examples showing how grading can be skewed by averaging grades on a 100-point scale as compared to a 4-point scale. For example, consider three students from the same class, all who earned a semester grade of "C" based on nine assessments averaged over an 18-week period (Figure 8.2).

Student Name	Test 1	Test 2	Test 3	Test 4	Test 5	Test 6	Test 7	Test 8	Test 9	Average	Grade
VanNessa	80	95	82	90	81	60	55	45	62	72.22	C
Malcolm	63	76	78	69	73	76	76	69	73	72.55	C
Destinee	100	100	0	99	50	100	0	98	98	71.66	C

Figure 8.2

While all three students earned the same grade, Destinee, who failed to turn in two assignments and turned another in late, clearly knows the material. VanNessa, who started the semester strong but then struggled, clearly does not. Sometimes different visual representations are helpful, so the same information provided strengthens the argument against averaging further (Figure 8.3).

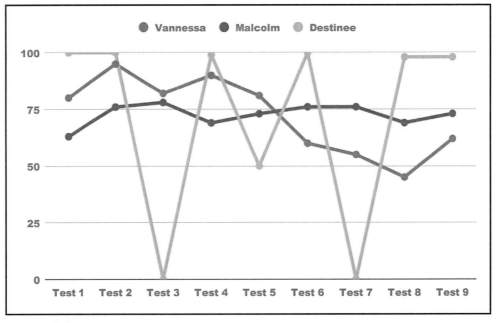

Figure 8.3

There is a wealth of information on grading, and there is simply not enough space here to go into depth about the topic. Let's ask a simple question: What do we really want a grade to represent? If you ask teachers, a vast majority of them are going to say that grades should represent academic achievement. When we look at actual practice in many high schools, however, we find a much different reality. Instead of being used as tools to report progress, grades are used as tools for compliance. They become tools of control and behavior modification, and are very poor tools for these purposes. Students who have received several zeros or poor grades with no opportunity to recover from them feel trapped, hopeless, inferior, and doomed. In light of those feelings, are students likely to suddenly turn the corner and become a model student? Unlikely. They are likely to check out and become even more disconnected and unmotivated than before (Reeves, 2011). Our goal as educators is to come up with a system that accurately represents students' progress and also gives them the chance to recover when they do poorly.

Making the Shift

In order to return our focus to learning and encourage students to take chances, the punitive qualities of grading and assessment simply must be eliminated; therefore, grading policies absolutely must include provisions for re-assessment and the opportunity to recover from poor performances. This doesn't mean teachers should forget about deadlines, accountability, or just give students the opportunity to repeatedly retest until they pass. In fact, nothing is less productive than allowing reassessment without some kind of extra effort being put in by the student to demonstrate they have learned what they need to know. Students must give their best effort on the first attempt and then show new evidence of learning before being re-assessed (Larson & Hierck, 2018). Teachers understandably worry about students procrastinating, failing to study, or otherwise slacking off because they know they will get another shot at the test. Reassessment done well, however, requires more work be done by students, not less, and they certainly learn more from the process than they would from a failing grade (Larson & Hierck, 2018). Making students show new evidence of learning makes sense from an educational standpoint because what we're talking about here is freeing students from the fear of failure and the stigma and negative impacts associated with high-stakes assessments or assignments.

Reassessment allows a student to do poorly on a specific assignment and yet recover once they demonstrate mastery. It's curious that so many in education feel that it is important for all students to learn exactly the same thing at exactly the same time. This is a ridiculous and impossible expectation that causes anxiety for our students and really makes no sense from an academic perspective.

For example, let's say the first unit in an Algebra class is simply learning how to solve for *x*. A student fails the test because she doesn't understand how to isolate the variable. In a school where retakes are not allowed, that student may never recover, because she has failed to master a basic algebraic skill. If, however, she is given some targeted intervention during her study hall period and is allowed to retake the test, she is likely to succeed and continue learning higher levels of math. This experience may suggest to the student that she needs to approach her math studies differently, do more homework, get assistance from a tutor on a regular basis, or simply pay better attention in class. She is unlikely to approach things the same way she did the first time because she had to do additional work to get caught up. Most importantly, our hypothetical student learned that doing poorly on something isn't the end of the world. She learned that focused perseverance yields results, and her teacher cared enough about her to provide additional opportunities for learning.

Some educators (although not many, fortunately) respond to these kinds of scenarios by saying things like, "She should have learned it the first time." Not only does this response show a fundamental ignorance of how the brain works, it demonstrates a naive view of a world where everyone can work at the same speed, understand at the same level, and experience the same initial success. Nowhere outside of schools are people expected to get it right the first time. Imagine a world where Thomas Edison has a great idea, and he goes to his lab to try it out. Improving on work done before him, he uses a filament that burns out after only a few moments. Edison realizes this method does not work, and he closes his shop and goes home. As he did not learn it the first time, he gives up and no longer has his invention. Does any inventor or engineer operate that way? Of course not. In actuality, Edison made thousands of attempts at the proper filament before he found the right one. It is vitally important that students realize getting it "right" the first time is not necessarily the goal. The goal is to learn how to persevere, work, and ultimately succeed.

Zeros and Late Work

There are several approaches that can be taken to address zeros, late work and punitive grading practices. Ultimately, it will be up to each individual school to decide what works for them. In some schools, a zero is simply replaced with an incomplete and a grade is not assigned until the work is completed. This provision applies for work that is fundamental to the course and is deemed essential by the teacher. For instance, if a student fails to turn in his compare/contrast essay, and if this essay is an essential element of the class, that student does not receive a grade for the quarter, semester, etc., until the assignment is done. The message sent is that every element of the curriculum is important and must be mastered in order to earn credit. Students who are adept at figuring out which assignments they can skip and still earn a passing grade are deprived of that option. This approach is radical, but can be effective. In one school, for example, this kind of policy resulted in significantly fewer students failing (Bafile, 2008).

In schools or departments that insist on continuing to assign zeros, switching to a 4-point scale is an option. The 4-point grading scale, which is easy to use in conjunction with different types of rubrics, weighs each grade equally, so assigning zeros doesn't result in the outsized impact seen on a 100-point scale. This is a difficult shift for some teachers, but not as drastic as a system that does not use incompletes. Students should still be given the opportunity to reassess when they struggle. Many researchers have written on this topic. Myron Dueck (2014), Thomas Guskey (2014), Doug Reeves (2011), and Rick Wormeli (2006) all have published resources full of both research and practical advice for school leaders wishing to move away from traditional grading models.

One of the most frustrating things teachers deal with is students' inability to consistently turn work in on time. Sometimes this is a result of student procrastination; sometimes it's due to circumstances beyond the student's control, and sometimes a student will actually do the work and forget to turn it in. How a teacher responds to late work should be consistent, fair, and preserve the integrity of the grading system. If the school's system claims to accurately reflect student learning, then full academic credit must be given when an assignment is turned in late. To do anything less would be to sabotage the grade as a measure of student learning.

For example, picture a student who works on a term paper for weeks. He finishes the assignment at 2:00 A.M. and goes to bed. When he gets to class and digs into his backpack, he realizes that his English folder is not there; perhaps he left it on his desk at home, along with his term paper. The teacher has a grading policy which automatically deducts 50% for late work, so the student's paper, which happens to be the most thoroughly-researched and most well-written in the class, earns an "F." Because this paper is the culminating assignment of the semester, the student's semester grade drops from an "A" to a "C." How does that student feel? Excited to write more excellent essays? Probably not. This does not mean students can't be accountable for deadlines. Marzano suggested that when students' work is turned in late, they must choose an additional task from a menu of options in order to demonstrate their learning (Marzano, 2006). Other schools may simply decide that deadlines should be more flexible, and that no consequence can be applied for late work.

Grading and assessment systems that encourage student perseverance and excellence do exist. Tom Guskey, an expert in grading and assessment, suggested a system of A/B/Not Yet as a viable option when speaking at a high school several years ago. In this system, students are held to a minimum standard of mastery and do not receive a grade until they reach it. When they demonstrated mastery, the grade is no less than a "B." If exemplary levels of mastery are demonstrated, the grade becomes an "A." Guskey's approach seems like a reasonable expectation—one in which students would be required to work hard to achieve clear objectives, but where the grade assigned becomes an indicator of mastery, rather than a goal in and of itself. It is also one in which students wouldn't be afraid to try, because "not yet" doesn't have the same negative connotations as an "F."

The grading discussion is a difficult one and one that many school leaders are hesitant to have. Fortunately, many teachers recognize the need to make changes in this area. They see the negative impact current grading systems and practices have on students and want to do better by them. For example, in our school, three veteran teachers decided to form a committee to look at the issue of grading practices. They started a conversation about what universal policies should be put into place as a school and which practices can be flexible based on department standards. As the process continued, we found ourselves asking what it would mean if fewer students failed and had to repeat courses? What would happen for students post-secondary options? How would it affect our school report card? Our standing in the community? These questions are similar to those that researcher pose when encountering shifts in grading systems and practices (Reeves, 2011).

Cultures of Learning vs. Cultures of Work

It is possible to create students who persevere through the instruction and guidance present in individual classrooms. Students are the product of the work going on in classroom spaces. By necessity, discussion moves from a more global lens to what goes on in classrooms every day. How can you develop students whose goal is not to simply avoid failure but develop students whose purpose is to grow, persevere, and succeed? There is a very big difference between those two mindsets, and ultimately, it is up to educators at all levels to help students embrace the necessary work to develop growth mindsets.

One of the most difficult things for high schools to come to grips with is how to motivate unmotivated students. We struggle to understand why students refuse to engage. Are they bored? Is the work too difficult for them? Is something going on at home? All of these things matter, and it is certainly important to make sure students are being challenged at the appropriate level and that their emotional needs are met (Rollins, 2014). What we suggest, however, is that motivation comes down to the culture found in each individual classroom. Consider assessing if the culture whether focused on *learning* or focused on *work*. There is a distinct difference between the two.

In a learning-centered classroom, emphasis is on understanding, problem-solving, arguments, debate, application, and creating rich environments where students talk about their thinking, how they are approaching things, why they are learning the content or skills, and why that knowledge or skill matters beyond the classroom. In a work-centered classroom, the focus is on activity—getting things done. Students are busy, and some of the activities may actually create understanding, but some may not. In a work-centered classroom, the teacher is the driver who is responsible for delivering the curriculum. Teachers in work-centered classrooms focus on what students need to do to finish the assignment.

In contrast, students in learning-centered classrooms focus on what type of thinking they will be required to do (Ritchhart, Church, & Morrison, 2011). If we want to truly transform our high schools, we need to shift away from work-centered rooms to more learning-centered ones.

Motivation

Another reason to adopt learning-centered classrooms is found in the benefit of engaging students in higher levels of motivation. Learning-centered classrooms encourage student investment because lessons are built around interesting tasks that give students an opportunity to observe closely, build explanations and interpretations, reason with evidence, make connections, consider different viewpoints, form their own conclusions, ask questions and uncover complexity by "going below the surface of things" (Ritchhart, Church, & Morrison, 2011, p.13). By contrast, a student in a work-centered classroom may find themselves doing things, but most of their activity focuses on surface-level learning. For example, during a recent classroom visit, we observed students drawing movie posters based on a book they had just read. Students were all busy. According to Charlotte Danielson's domain 3C, the "engagement" of students may likely be demonstrated by the educator; however, the lesson fell flat for a number of reasons, the first being that it offered students no real choices. Creating a movie poster was their only option. The lesson didn't ask the students to think deeply about their reading; simple understanding of a scene and a character was enough to complete the assignment, so the task itself lacked challenge and interest. Consequently, the students saw it as busy work and reacted accordingly.

In order to foster perseverance in students, tasks must be both meaningful and challenging. To meet these requirements, teachers have to release responsibility for learning to the students. This is difficult for many teachers, but it is absolutely essential if students are going to learn reasoning skills and solve problems on their own. Understandably, teachers feel pressure to get through approved curriculum, and they also feel a pressing need for students to succeed. The result can be a very teacher-centric approach. One of the keys to student motivation, however, is giving students a choice. Even minor choices can lead to more motivation on the part of students and can increase investment in a task significantly (Rollins, 2014). Rather than assigning all students the same task, for example, the teacher can present a menu of options, or, depending on the class, provide some guidelines within which to work while allowing students to come up with their own approach to demonstrate their mastery of a specific skill. This approach requires students to think creatively, which may then generate more interest and deeper understanding, not to mention greater motivation.

When planning, teachers need to explicitly define exactly what they are looking to accomplish in each lesson. Some sample questions they can ask themselves are presented below.

1. **Why am I doing this activity?** This question gets at the root of motivating students, and can be uncomfortable for teachers to ask, especially if they have been doing a particular lesson for a long time and it turns out to have little academic or relational value. Perhaps

they will discover the reason for doing the activity isn't worth the class time that it will take, or that it is busy work.

2. **Why am I using this method in my learning activity?** Going back to the movie poster example, if the teacher had considered this question, she may have realized that little learning was going to be generated by the activity.

3. **What kind of thinking am I trying to engage?** This is a question that teachers need to ask themselves regularly. Decisions should be made about whether they're looking for analysis, interpretation, metacognition, connection, reasoning, drawing conclusions, etc. The kind of thinking engaged helps the teacher determine what activity or approach is most appropriate.

4. **How am I challenging student thinking?** Teachers should always plan ahead for several essential questions that will challenge student assumptions and push them to higher levels of thinking. These kinds of questions create both interest and inquiry; answering them allows students to flex their intellectual muscle (Wiggins & McTighe, 2013).

5. **How are students challenging their own thinking?** Students should be constantly reminded that their thinking is valuable. By examining how they are thinking about things and why they are coming to the conclusions they are, students learn the valuable skill of metacognition.

By asking questions such as these, teachers can recognize what they want to accomplish in students' learning as opposed to focusing on a series of activities to be completed prior to a test. From a student perspective, lessons crafted with these questions in mind should result in more meaningful experiences. Ultimately, this process ends with an increase in student motivation and engagement.

Aligning the Pieces

In this chapter, we attempted to frame a process for students who are resilient, who can overcome adversity and who persevere to the point where they succeed. In order to develop students with these skills, an understanding of the importance of failure is required, as well as creating school environments where students are motivated by learning rather than rewards. Students who persevere are motivated by meaningful, interesting tasks, and they thrive in environments where they make choices about their learning. In order to foster an environment where perseverance is rewarded, schools must explore their structures and practices to ensure students have the opportunity to recover when they don't do well and are recognized for their efforts when they do.

9 ALIGNING ALL THE PIECES TO MAKE REAL CHANGE

In human affairs of danger and delicacy successful conclusion is sharply limited by hurry.

- John Steinbeck

There are fundamental truths that emerge over the course of a career in education. First, the work of educating children is complicated, challenging, and incredibly rewarding. Second, change is extremely difficult. This chapter will help you begin a plan for creating a vision and starting your change process.

Vision: Where Do You Want to Be?

After coming to an understanding about what your school does well, and then committing to maintaining and communicating those successes, it is time to purposefully identify exactly where you want to be. The process is more difficult than it might seem, but it is essential to developing a plan that will succeed.

Any group of administrators can come up with a goal. The real challenge lies in creating a unifying and compelling vision. Some schools mistakenly use improving test scores as their primary vision, but this is misguided. Test scores are important, especially because so much stock is invested in grading schools and showing accountability; however, improving test scores is not a *vision*. It does nothing to energize your school or give you a sense of purpose. More important, simply improving test scores will not truly change your school. There is plenty of research pointing to the negligible effects that test scores have on success (Berliner & Glass, 2014; Zhao, 2016). It is clear that focusing solely on that area will not lead to meaningful change.

We propose creating a vision that everyone in your building can be proud of, one that is easily communicated and can be measured. The vision should also be tailored to your specific situation. It should be realistic—challenging, but attainable.

When leaders sit down to look at goals, we're tempted to throw things out there like, "We want our school to be the best high school in the state!" Great. That is certainly a laudable goal. After all, who wouldn't want to be the best high school in their state? The problem is, this goal is pretty tough to measure, and even harder to accomplish. What determines the *best* high school? Test scores, programs, participation? Would an urban school housing a high percentage of disadvantaged students realistically be able to surpass the "best" schools that can recruit students and/or require a test score to enter? Would those urban schools compare favorably to suburban ones populated by wealthy students having access to tutors, test prep services, private coaches, and unlimited resources? The answer to these questions is probably not, although we would argue that an urban school could come pretty close to more affluent schools if the measures were student academic growth, development of a sense of self-worth, and a commitment to community service.

What if the vision were, "We want to be the best large, diverse high school in the state," and then we developed some criteria for determining *best*? These could include test scores, growth scores, participation in athletics and clubs, and opportunities to take honors/AP classes. By establishing criteria, the vision becomes more attainable. Another example could be, "All students who graduate from our large, diverse high school will have options for pursuing whatever post-secondary endeavor they desire?" Too broad? Maybe, but it *is* measurable through various metrics.

When developing your vision, perhaps the most important question to consider is *why*. *Why* do you feel this is appropriate for your school? After all, you are going to be dedicating research, time, and professional capital toward reaching it, so you better have some thought about why this is your compelling vision. Also, partnering with your board of education and your community on supporting your vision will require the capacity to articulate *why* it is so important and *why* it will benefit your students.

The Change Process

Once a vision has been created and articulated, school leaders must then plan and implement a process for making their vision a reality. The change process is difficult, which is why so much literature has been devoted to it. Many authors and researchers have written about ways in which leaders can successfully approach change. For example, John Kotter suggested eight specific steps in the change process. These eight steps can be grouped into three phases: creating a climate for change, engaging and enabling the entire organization, and implementing and sustaining change (Kotter, 1996). Similarly, Douglas Reeves also cited three things that must happen before change can occur: dispelling myths, leveraging leadership for change, and planning for change (Reeves, 2009). Fullan also presented three specific components to the change process: Initiation, Implementation, and Institutionalization, with Institutionalization representing the time where a change has become an integral part of the school's functioning (Fullan, 2007). An exhaustive examination of the change process is not necessary for our purposes, but leaders are certainly encouraged to read these theories and apply their principles as appropriate for their situations. For our purposes, we hope you will begin by revisiting and considering the four entry points to change that we believe are critical to rethinking your school, as presented in Chapters 3 through 6:

- Structure (Chapter 3)
- Curriculum (Chapter 4)
- Instruction (Chapter 5)
- Culture (Chapter 6)

Getting Started

Sometimes it seems as if educational institutions only exist in two states: complete inertia or frenzied activity. Frenzied activity can be seen in this familiar scenario: an administrator goes to a conference, picks up a new idea, and then comes back to the school and implements it. The next year, she goes to another conference, talks with an impressive vendor, and then comes back to school and adopts that vendor's program before the previous year's initiative ever takes hold. There are few things more damaging to a school than a state of frantic, unfocused, and directionless activity. While both frenzied activity and inertia are counterproductive, of the two, inertia is probably the more prevalent and persistent.

> Inertia /ɪˈnəːʃə/ (noun):
>
> 1. A tendency to do nothing or to remain unchanged. 'the bureaucratic inertia of the various tiers of government'

The state of inertia is where educators rest safe in the satisfaction and knowledge that what has been will always be. It is understandable why the simple act of doing nothing can become so easy. Regardless of how dedicated or hardworking they are, there is simply a limit to how many things that staff can be asked to do. As a result, even the most well-intended and designed program is prone to failure due to what Doug Reeves termed *initiative fatigue* (Reeves, 2014). Over the course of their careers, teachers and administrators are relentlessly bombarded with new initiatives, standards, accountability measures, and an onslaught of standardized tests. As a result, a "this too shall pass" mentality permeates many schools. This is understandable, but school leaders cannot make excuses for accepting the status quo, and educators cannot simply accept the state of inertia. On the other hand, it is critical that effective school leaders not become like so many before them and simply fly by the seat of their pants in the misguided hope that something which is thrown in the general direction of a target will somehow stick.

Perhaps the real reason inertia can be such a problem in schools is the simple tendency to be overwhelmed by all of the things needing to be accomplished. Depending on individual circumstances, some schools and districts have more to do than others, but all are faced with unique and difficult challenges such as academics, culture, poverty, community struggles, and (increasingly) mental health. In the face of everything that needs doing, it is often difficult to understand exactly where to start. In the search for a perfect data-driven solution, educators find themselves delving into test scores, surveys, and other mounds of data and then struggling to understand what to do with it all. The result is a kind a paralysis by analysis, a collective spinning of wheels that does nobody any good. Don't believe it? Make a list of all the data that your school district collects, and then honestly assess what percentage of it is *actually* put to good use. You may be surprised by the result.

The important thing is not that you start in exactly the right place but that you *start*. We are reminded of the Chinese proverb: "The journey of a thousand miles begins with a single step." Our goal here is ensuring that your single step is not backwards, sideways, or in any other direction that takes you further from your goal. The first and most obvious task that you must commit to is *starting*. As you begin, understand that re-imagining a large organization can be like turning a battleship. The sheer size of the task can make it happen slower than you might want, and other factors will play into your task as well. For example, a ship turning against a strong tide or a vicious headwind will have to work harder, and perhaps longer, to get pointed in the right direction. It is essential that administrators understand their own unique situations and plan accordingly.

What Do You Do Well?

Determining your vision is difficult and essential. Once the vision is created, it is still easy to get lost in the minutiae, or to become so specific that the overall vision becomes obscured by meaningless and distracting detail. In order to maintain a zealous focus on your school's vision, we suggest beginning with an accounting of what your school does really well. By understanding where your school is strong, you can use those strengths to maintain a positive school culture while forming the foundation for the new vision you are trying to build. The following Living Narrative illustrates that process.

Living Narrative

Imagine a large suburban high school where both demographics and size changed dramatically over the years. In the late 1980s, there were about 2,500 students in the school. Of these, roughly 70% were White, 10% were Hispanic, and 20% were Black. The low-income rate was 10%, and only 1% of students were limited English speakers. Thirty years later, the population has grown to about 3,700 students. Now, 30% of students are White, 55% are Hispanic, and 10% are Black. Low-income students represent 56% of the population, and English language learners make up 10% of the student body. The commu-

nity is home to a refugee resettlement program, and 56 different languages are spoken by students. An organization serving the homeless is also located within school boundaries, as is a facility for students who have been orphaned, or have been removed from their homes after being abused. In addition to the demographic shifts, the high school has had seven different principals over the last decade.

As a new principal and leadership team begin to assess the school and what they want it to become, they first take the time to understand what is special about their school. First and foremost, they focus on the students. They find the students to be persistent and compassionate. While many of them come from hard circumstances, they care for each other like no other students the leadership team has ever been around. They also possess an exceptional spirit of volunteerism and empathy. Most of all, the students are very proud of their school.

The second thing the new team sees as a strength is history and tradition. The school is one of the oldest in the state, and students are proud of being part of a legacy spanning 150 years. Part of this legacy is the school's diversity. While it has certainly become more diverse in the past 10-15 years, the high school has always been a place where students of all races, colors, and creeds have worked, studied, and played together. The new team recognizes their students' ability to work with those unlike themselves, and they consider it to be a decided advantage for students when entering a global workplace.

Last, but certainly not least, the new team sees a school boasting a truly exceptional Fine Arts program. The marching band fields 300 members during every home football game; there are four different extracurricular jazz bands, several extracurricular choirs, and a full contingent of academic band and choir classes. The Visual Arts program, which was named the top program in the state, offers classes in drawing, painting, ceramics, sculpture, photography, digital art, and animation. Students have the opportunity to pursue their interests in the performing arts both during the school day in drama classes, which include instruction in both performance and technical aspects of theatre such as lighting and set design, as well as through acting, performing, and producing professional-quality theatrical shows widely attended by community members... many whom have no other connections to the school.

As the new principal and leadership team recognized all of the things that their school did well, they also saw a responsibility to both protect and strengthen these facets as they moved to improve in other areas. Whatever their ultimate goal turned out to be, part of it had to be preserving the things that make their school the amazing place that it was. They realized that it does a school no good to improve test scores if the soul of the enterprise is lost. As part of their mission, the leadership team committed to one additional responsibility: communicating the many successes experienced by their students every day in order to counter the inevitable negative perceptions associated with the current environment of accountability.

Purpose and Belief

By examining the current state of high schools as a product of historical trends and forces, it is clear school leaders may feel like a battered ship at sea. Due to constantly changing areas of focus, punitive mandates, shifting targets of success, and scathing rhetoric, it is no wonder that schools feel demoralized and at a loss for how to proceed. As we have advocated throughout this book, we believe that success for each student and each school is unique and therefore needs to be constructed with the support and buy in of all the stakeholders invested in the success of a school. Unfortunately, the things for which many schools are held accountable do not capture everything high schools do to ensure students are college and career ready.

High school leaders and stakeholders are wise to begin by defining the vision for their school, their staff, their students and community at large. In the absence of a unifying purpose, schools can fall prey to others projecting their disconnected purposes upon the school. When schools are burdened with many unrealistic and competing agendas, they risk disappointing everyone. We hope that this book helps you define your purpose, articulate your vision, create your plan, and find your focus to broadcast to all who will listen. By articulating a purpose and vision with aligned goals, leaders are able to proceed with clarity.

High schools are places in which unique, interesting, and complicated young adults learn, grow, challenge themselves, and contribute every day. Imposing business models of accountability and simplistic criteria of evaluation upon schools limits our ability to recognize the truly amazing things that happen in high schools every day. By trying to lump all of the desired outputs of high school into scores or grades, we may miss the opportunity to witness and celebrate the amazing things that happen. If we can find a focus that allows us to acknowledge the unique (and sometimes unmeasurable) things that are truly valuable, then we allow for more opportunity to believe in ourselves and our students. This does not happen overnight. It is difficult to create the space for individualized and evolving forms of success; however, without that discretionary space, schools will fall victim to narrow and constricting paradigms of success that are not healthy or robust enough to serve our students and communities properly.

The work of rethinking your high school is not easy. The work of changing your high school may seem completely overwhelming. We hope that we have energized you to tackle that work. While all challenges are unique, we hope that you are now prepared to consider a variety of philosophical and action-based approaches to improving the high school you work in. While your plan and approach will look different than anyone else's, it is vital to remember that you cannot do it alone; others want to help, and success breeds more success.

REFERENCES

Akos, P., & Galassi, J. P. (2004). Middle and high school transitions as viewed by students, parents, and teachers. *Professional School Counseling*, *7*(4), 212-221.

Alspaugh, J. W. (1998). Achievement loss associated with the transition to middle school and high school. *Journal of Educational Research*, *92*(1), 20-25.

Aronson, J., Fried, C. B., & Good, C. (2002). Reducing the effects of stereotype threat on African American college students by shaping theories of intelligence. *Journal of Experimental Social Psychology*, *38*(2), 113-125.

Bafile, C. (2008, August 18). *Teaching heroes: Toss the zeros.* Retrieved from https://www.educationworld.com/a_admin/admin/admin531.shtml

Bandura, A. (1977). Self-efficacy: Toward a unifying theory of behavioral change. *Psychological Review*, *84*(2), 191.

Bandura, A. (1994). Self-efficacy. In V. S. Ramachaudran, *Encyclopedia of human behavior*, *4*(4), 71-81.

Baskin, S. (2011, December 3). *The gift of failure: Letting our children struggle is a difficult gift to give.* Retrieved from https://www.psychologytoday.com/us/b;g/smores-and-more/201112/ the-gift-failure

Baumeister, R. F., Campbell, J. D., Krueger, J. I., & Vohs, K. D. (2003). Does high self-esteem cause better performance, interpersonal success, happiness, or healthier lifestyles? *Psychological Science in the Public Interest*, *4*(1), 1-44.

Berliner, D. C., & Biddle, B. J. (1996). The manufactured crisis: Myths, fraud, and the attack on America's public schools. *NASSP Bulletin*, *80*(576), 119-121.

Berliner, D. C., & Glass, G. V. (Eds.). (2014). *50 myths and lies that threaten America's public schools: The real crisis in education*. New York, NY: Teachers College Press.

Blad, E. (2015). Teachers nurture growth mindsets in math. *Education Week, 35*(3), 1-11.

Bolman, L. G., & Deal, T. E. (2003). *Reframing organizations*. San Francisco, CA: Jossey-Bass.

Boyd, D., Grossman, P., Ing, M., Lankford, H., Loeb, S., & Wyckoff, J. (2011). The influence of school administrators on teacher retention decisions. *American Educational Research Journal, 48*(2), 303-333.

Bracey, G. W. (2003). April foolishness: The 20th anniversary of A Nation at Risk. *Phi Delta Kappan, 84*(8), 616-621.

Bracey, G. W. (2008). Cut scores, NAEP achievement levels and their discontents. *School Administrator, 65*(6), 20-23.

Bracey, G. W. (2008). On the shortage of scientists and engineers. *Phi Delta Kappan, 89*(7), 536-538.

Bracey, G. W. (2008). Disastrous legacy: Aftermath of a nation at risk. *Dissent, 55*(4), 80-83.

Brame, C. J. (2015). Effective educational videos. *Vanderbilt University Center for Teaching*.

Bryant, J. (2012). *America's next education crisis—and who benefits*. Retrieved from http://www. washingtonpost.com/news/answer-sheet/wp/2012/12/07/americas-next-education-crisis-and-who-benefits/

Burris, C. C., & Welner, K. G. (2005). Closing the achievement gap by detracking. *Phi Delta Kappan, 86*(8), 594-598.

Bushaw, W. J., & Lopez, S. J. (2013). Which way do we go? *Phi Delta Kappan, 95*(1), 8-25.

Butts, M. J., & Cruzeiro, P. A. (2005). Student perceptions of factors leading to an effective transition from eighth to ninth grade. *American Secondary Education, 34*(1), 70-80.

Cazden, C. B. (2001). *Classroom discourse: The language of teaching and learning*. Portsmouth, NH: Heinemann.

Cauley, K. M., & Jovanovich, D. (2006). Developing an effective transition program for students entering middle school or high school. *The Clearing House: A Journal of Educational Strategies, Issues and Ideas, 80*(1), 15-25.

Chen, G. (2017). *A relevant history of public education in the United States*. Retrieved from https://www.publicschoolreview.com/blog/a-relevant-history-of-public-education-in-the-united-states

Chen, X. (2016). *Remedial coursetaking at US public 2-and 4-year institutions: Scope, experiences, and outcomes (Statistical Analysis Report. NCES 2016-405).* Washington, DC: National Center for Education Statistics.

Christmas, D., Kudzai, C., & Josiah, M. (2013). Vygotsky's zone of proximal development theory: What are its implications for mathematical teaching? *Greener Journal of Social Sciences, 3*(7), 371-377.

Cooney, S., Moore, B., & Bottoms, G. (2002). Gaps to close to prep them for high school. *The Education Digest, 67*(8), 44.

Danielson, C. (2011). *Enhancing professional practice: A framework for teaching.* Alexandria, VA: ASCD.

Darling-Hammond, L. (2007). Race, inequality and educational accountability: The irony of "No Child Left Behind." *Race Ethnicity and Education, 10*(3), 245-260.

Deci, E. L., Koestner, R., & Ryan, R. M. (1999). A meta-analytic review of experiments examining the effects of extrinsic rewards on intrinsic motivation. *Psychological Bulletin, 125*(6), 627.

Dee, T. S., & Jacob, B. (2011). The impact of No Child Left Behind on student achievement. *Journal of Policy Analysis and Management, 30*(3), 418-446.

DePree, M. (1988). *Leadership is an art.* New York, NY: Bantam Doubleday Dell.

Donohoo, J. (2017). Collective teacher efficacy research: implications for professional learning. *Journal of Professional Capital and Community, 2*(2), 101-116.

Dueck, M. (2014). *Grading smarter, not harder: Assessment strategies that motivate kids and help them learn.* Alexandria, VA: ASCD.

Dufour, R. (2007 January 29). *Why educators should be given the time to collaborate.* Retrieved from http://www.allthingsplc.info/blog/view/3/why-educators-should-be-given-time-to-collaborate

DuFour, R., & Fullan, M. (2013). *Cultures built to last: Systemic PLCs at work.* Bloomington, IN: Solution Tree Press.

Durm, M. W. (1993, September). An A is not an A is not an A: A history of grading. *Educational Forum, 57*(3), 294-297.

Dweck, C. S. (2008). *Mindset: The new psychology of success.* New York, NY: Random House Digital.

Dweck, C. S., Walton, G. M., & Cohen, G. L. (2014). *Academic tenacity: Mindsets and skills that promote long-term learning.* Seattle, WA: Bill & Melinda Gates Foundation.

Dwyer, W. (2017). *Principal self-efficacy: A qualitative exploration* (Doctoral dissertation, Northern Illinois University).

Erskine, J. L. (2014). It changes how teachers teach: How testing is corrupting our classrooms and student learning. *Multicultural Education, 21*(2), 38-40.

Evidence Based Funding for Student Success Act, Illinois Public Act 100-0465 (2017). Retrieved from http://www.ilga.gov/legislation/publicacts/fulltext.asp?Name=100-0465

Fabricant, M., & Fine, M. (2015). *Charter schools and the corporate makeover of public education: What's at stake?* New York, NY: Teachers College Press.

Fink, J., Jenkins, D., & Yanagiura, T. (2017). *What happens to students who take community college "dual enrollment" courses in high school?* New York, NY: Community College Research Center, Teachers College, Columbia University.

Finkelstein, I. E. (1913). *The marking system in theory and practice* (No. 10). Baltimore, MD: Warwick & York.

Flank, L. (2015). *Space race: Why the US let the soviets win.* Retrieved from https://lflank.wordpress.com/2015/07/15/space-race-why-the-us-let-the-soviets-win/

Frey, N., Fisher, D., & Hattie, J. (2018). Developing "assessment capable" learners. *Educational Leadership, 75*(5), 46-51.

Fullan, H. (2007). *The new meaning of educational change: Causes and processes of implementation and continuation.* New York, NY: Teachers College Press.

Fullan, M. (2018). *The principal: Three keys to maximizing impact.* Malden, MA: John Wiley & Sons.

Goddard, R. D., Hoy, W. K., & Hoy, A. W. (2000). Collective teacher efficacy: Its meaning, measure, and impact on student achievement. *American Educational Research Journal, 37*(2), 479-507.

Guskey, T. R. (2014). *On your mark: Challenging the conventions of grading and reporting.* Bloomington, IN: Solution Tree Press.

Goodpasture, A. J. (1957). Memorandum of Conference with President Eisenhower, October 8. 1957, 8:30 am (National Archives Catalog document # 186623). Retrieved from https://catalog.archives.gov/id/186623

Hattie, J. (2008). *Visible learning: A synthesis of over 800 meta-analyses relating to achievement.* London, England: Routledge.

Hattie, J. (2012). *Visible learning for teachers: Maximizing impact on learning.* London, England: Routledge.

Hattie, J. (2015). *What works best in education: The politics of collaborative expertise.* Upper Saddle River, NJ: Pearson.

Hattie, J., & Zierer, K. (2018). *Ten mindframes for visible learning: Teaching for success.* London, England: Routledge Taylor & Francis Group.

Helgerson, J. L. (1996). *CIA briefings of presidential candidates.* Washington, DC: CIA.

Henderson, S. (2016, December 3). Betsy DeVos and the twilight of public education. *Detroit Free Press.* Retrieved from https://www.freep.com/story/opinion/columnists/stephen-henderson/2016/12/03/betsy-devos-education-donald-trump/94728574/

Herold, J. (1974). Sputnik in American education: A history and reappraisal. *McGill Journal of Education/Revue des sciences de l'éducation de McGill, 9*(002).

Howerton, A. M. (2016). *Elephant on a stepladder: An exploration of pre-service English teacher assessment literacy* (Doctoral dissertation, Northern Illinois University).

Hoy, W. K., Sweetland, S. R., & Smith, P. A. (2002). Toward an organizational model of achievement in high schools: The significance of collective efficacy. *Educational Administration Quarterly, 38*(1), 77-93.

Hunt, J. W. (2008). A Nation at Risk and No Child Left Behind: Déjà vu for administrators? *Phi Delta Kappan, 89*(8), 580-585.

Illinois Public Act 100-0465 (2017).

Johnson, D. W., Johnson, R. T., & Stanne, M. B. (2000). Cooperative learning methods: A meta-analysis.

Kagan, S. (1989). The structural approach to cooperative learning. *Educational Leadership, 47*(4), 12-15.

Knight, J. (2011). *Unmistakable impact.* Thousand Oaks, CA: Corwin Press.

Kohn, A. (1994). The truth about self-esteem. *Phi Delta Kappan, 76,* 272-272.

Kotter, J. P. (1996). *Leading change.* Boston, MA: Harvard Business School Press.

Leithwood, K., & Jantzi, D. (2008). Linking leadership to student learning: The contributions of leader efficacy. *Educational Administration Quarterly, 44*(4), 496-528.

Lin-Siegler, X., Dweck, C. S., & Cohen, G. L. (2016). Instructional interventions that motivate classroom learning. *Journal of Educational Psychology, 108*(3), 295.

Markow, D., & Pieters, A. (2012). *The MetLife survey of the American teacher: Teachers, parents and the economy.* New York, NY: MetLife.

Marzano, R. J. (2003). *What works in schools: Translating research into action.* Alexandria, VA: ASCD.

Marzano, R. J. (2006). *Classroom assessment & grading that work*. Alexandria, VA: ASCD.

Marzano, R. J. (2007). *The art and science of teaching: A comprehensive framework for effective instruction*. Alexandria, VA: ASCD.

Marzano, R. J., Frontier, T., & Livingston, D. (2011). *Effective supervision: Supporting the art and science of teaching*. Alexandria, VA: ASCD.

Marzano, R. J., Waters, T., & McNulty, B. A. (2005). *School leadership that works: From research to results*. Alexandria, VA: ASCD.

Masters, D., Birch, K., & Hattie, J. (2015). *Visible learning into action: International case studies of impact*. Thousand Oaks, CA: Corwin Press.

Maxwell, J. C. (2007). *Failing forward*. New York, NY: Harper Collins.

McCallumore, K. M., & Sparapani, E. F. (2010). The importance of the ninth grade on high school graduation rates and student success in high school. *Education, 130*(3), 447-456.

McTighe, J., & Wiggins, G. (2013). *Essential questions: Opening doors to student understanding*. Alexandria, VA: ASCD.

Meier, D., & Knoester, M. (2017). *Beyond testing: Seven assessments of students and schools more effective than standardized tests*. New York, NY: Teachers College Press.

Muhammad, A. (2015). *Overcoming the achievement gap trap: Liberating mindsets to effect change*. Bloomington, IN: Solution Tree Press.

Myers-Briggs Type Indicator. (2018). Retrieved from https://www.myersbriggs.org/type-use-for-everyday-life/mbti-type-at-work/

Neild, R. C., Balfanz, R., & Herzog, L. (2007). An early warning system. *Educational Leadership, 65*(2), 28-33.

National Commission on Excellence in Education. (1983). A nation at risk: The imperative for educational reform. *Elementary School Journal, 84*(2), 113-130.

National Conference of Bar Examiners. (2019). *Bar admission guide*. Retrieved from http://www.ncbex.org/publications/bar-admissions-guide/

Nottingham, J. (2017). *Challenging learning*. Thousand Oaks, CA: Corwin Press.

Nottingham, J. (2017). *The learning challenge: How to guide your students through the learning pit to achieve deeper understanding*. Thousand Oaks, CA: Corwin Press.

Oakes, J. (2005). *Keeping track*. New Haven, CT: Yale University Press.

Ogbu, J. U. (1992). Adaptation to minority status and impact on school success. *Theory Into Practice, 31*(4), 287-295.

Oslington, G. (2018, August 11). Why failure helps gifted children achieve so much more. *The Sydney Morning Herald.* Retrieved from https://www.smh.com.au/education/why-failure-helps-gifted-children-achieve-so-much-more-20180806-h13le0.html

Page, C. (2019, March 15). College admission scandal reveals "status anxiety" run amok. *The Chicago Tribune.* Retrieved from https://www.chicagotribune.com

Pink, D. H. (2011). *Drive: The surprising truth about what motivates us.* New York, NY: Penguin.

Preble, C. A. (2003). "Who ever believed in the 'missile gap'?": John F. Kennedy and the politics of national security. *Presidential Studies Quarterly, 33*(4), 801-826.

Rado, D. (2016, July 12). Illinois ends much-debated PARCC test for high school students. *The Chicago Tribune.* Retrieved from http://www.chicagotribune.com/news/local/breaking/ctparcc-test-high-school-met-20160711-story.html

Ravitch, D. (2010). Why I changed my mind. *The Nation, 27*(1), 1-4.

Ravitch, D. (2011). Dictating to the schools. *The Education Digest, 76*(8), 4.

Ravitch, D. (2013). *Reign of error: The hoax of the privatization movement and the danger to America's public schools.* New York, NY: Vintage.

Ravitch, D., & Kohn, A. (2014). *More than a score: The new uprising against high-stakes testing.* Chicago, IL: Haymarket Books.

Reeves, D. B. (2004). *Accountability for learning: How teachers and school leaders can take charge.* Alexandria, VA: ASCD.

Reeves, D. B. (2009). *Leading change in your school: How to conquer myths, build commitment, and get results.* Alexandria, VA: ASCD.

Reeves, D. (2011). *Elements of grading: A guide to effective practice.* Bloomington, IN: Solution Tree Press.

Reeves, D. (2014). *Transforming professional development into student results.* Alexandria, VA: ASCD.

Ritchhart, R., Church, M., & Morrison, K. (2011). *Making thinking visible: How to promote engagement, understanding, and independence for all learners.* Malden, MA: John Wiley & Sons.

Roberts, T. P., & Zigarmi, D. (2014). The impact of dispositional cynicism on job-specific affect and work intentions. *International Journal of Psychology, 49*(5), 381-389.

Robinson, K. (2015). *How schools kill creativity.* Retrieved from https://creativesystemsthinking.wordpress.com/2015/04/26/ken-robinson-how-schools-kill-creativity/

Rollins, S. P. (2014). *Learning in the fast lane: 8 ways to put all students on the road to academic success.* Alexandria, VA: ASCD.

Rshaid, G. (2011). *Learning for the future: Rethinking schools for the 21st century.* Englewood, CO: Lead+Learn Press.

Sanders, W. L., & Rivers, J. C. (1996). *Cumulative and residual effects of teachers on future student academic achievement* (Research Progress Report). Knoxville, TN: University of Tennessee Value-Added Research and Assessment Center.

Schmoker, M. (2018). *Focus: Elevating the essentials to radically improve student learning.* Alexandria, VA: ASCD.

Schneider, J. (2017). *Beyond test scores: A better way to measure school quality.* Cambridge, MA: Harvard University Press.

Schwartz, M. S., Sadler, P. M., Sonnert, G., & Tai, R. H. (2009). Depth versus breadth: How content coverage in high school science courses relates to later success in college science coursework. *Science Education, 93*(5), 798-826.

Seed, A. H. (2008). Redirecting the teaching profession in the wake of a nation at risk and NCLB. *Phi Delta Kappan, 89*(8), 586-589.

Simon, S. (2015, February). *No profit left behind.* Retrieved from https://www.politico.com/story/2015/02/pearson-education-115026

Slavin, R. E. (1996). Research on cooperative learning and achievement: What we know, what we need to know. *Contemporary Educational Psychology, 21*(1), 43-69.

Smith, J. B. (1997). Effects of eighth-grade transition programs on high school retention and experiences. *Journal of Educational Research, 90*(3), 144-152.

Smith, J. S., Feldwisch, R., & Abell, A. (2006). Similarities and differences in students' and parents' perceptions of the transition from middle school to high school. *RMLE Online, 29*(10), 1-9.

Stiggins, R. J. (1991). Assessment literacy. *Phi Delta Kappan, 72*(7), 534-39.

Stiggins, R. J. (2004). New assessment beliefs for a new school mission. *Phi Delta Kappan, 86*(1), 22-27.

The 50th Annual PDK Poll of the Public's Attitudes Toward the Public Schools. (2018). *Phi Delta Kappan, 100*(1). doi:10.1177/0031721718797117

Taylor, R. T. (2010). Leadership to improve student achievement: Focus the culture on learning. *Journal of Scholarship and Practice, 7*(1), 10-23.

Tomlinson, C. A. (1999). Mapping a route toward differentiated instruction. *Educational Leadership, 57*, 12-17.

Venables, D. R. (2017). *Facilitating teacher teams and authentic PLCs: The human side of leading people, protocols, and practices.* Alexandria, VA: ASCD.

Watters, A. (2015). *The invented history of "The factory model of education."* Retrieved from http://hackeducation.com/2015/04/25/factory-model

Weissbourd, R., Thacker, L., Anderson, T. R., Cashin, A., Feigenberg, L. F., & Kahn, J. (2016). *Turning the tide: Inspiring concern for others and the common good through college admissions.* Retrieved from http://mcc.gse.harvard.edu/files/gsemcc/files/20160120 _mcc_ttt_report_interactive.pdf

Wiggins, G. (2012). Seven keys to effective feedback. *ASCD.* Retrieved from http://www.ascd.org/publications/educational-leadership/sept12/vol70/num01/Seven-Keys-to-Effective-Feedback.aspx

Wormeli, R. (2006). Accountability: Teaching through assessment and feedback, not grading. *American Secondary Education*, 14-27.

Yager, S., Johnson, R. T., Johnson, D. W., & Snider, B. (1986). The impact of group processing on achievement in cooperative learning groups. *Journal of Social Psychology*, *126*(3), 389-397.

Zhao, Y. (2009). *Catching up or leading the way: American education in the age of globalization.* Alexandria, VA: ASCD.

Zhao, Y. (2012). *World class learners: Educating creative and entrepreneurial students.* Thousand Oaks, CA: Corwin Press.

Zhao, Y. (2014). *Who's afraid of the big bad dragon? Why China has the best (and worst) education system in the world.* Malden, MA: John Wiley & Sons.

Zhao, Y. (Ed.). (2016). *Counting what counts: Reframing education outcomes.* Bloomington, IN: Solution Tree Press.

Zhao, Y. (2018, October 4). Comments at ILASCD conference, Naperville, Illinois.